The Siege of Malta
1940–1942

Campaign Chronicles

The Siege of Malta 1940–1942

David Williamson

Campaign Chronicles
Series Editor

Christopher Summerville

Pen & Sword
MILITARY

To Sue, Alex, Sarah and Antonia with thanks for their
help and encouragement

First published in Great Britain in 2007 by
Pen & Sword Military
an imprint of
Pen & Sword Books Ltd
47 Church Street
Barnsley
South Yorkshire S70 2AS

ISBN 978 1 84415 477 7

Typeset in Sabon by
Phoenix Typesetting, Auldgirth, Dumfriesshire

Printed and bound in England by
Biddles Ltd, King's Lynn

Pen & Sword Books Ltd incorporates the Imprints of Pen & Sword Aviation,
Pen & Sword Maritime, Pen & Sword Military, Wharncliffe Local History,
Pen & Sword Select, Pen & Sword Military Classics and Leo Cooper.

For a complete list of Pen & Sword titles please contact
PEN & SWORD BOOKS LIMITED
47 Church Street, Barnsley, South Yorkshire, S70 2AS, England
E-mail: enquiries@pen-and-sword.co.uk
Website: www.pen-and-sword.co.uk

Contents

The Siege of Malta

Plates

———◆———

The Siege of Malta

Maps

(pages x to xiv)

Acknowledgements

Sincerest thanks is due to the following individuals and websites for support in compiling the illustration scheme for this book: Tim Addis, Louis Henwood, Bill Lazell, Peter Norman, Rita Lyons, Jennie Crawford, Mr C.A. Rowntree, www.killifish.f9.co.uk, www.Louishenwood.com

The publisher has tried without success to contact the copyright holders of some of the illustrations, and would be pleased to hear from any untraced source.

The author would like to thank the following for granting him permission to use coyright material within their possession: Mrs M. Rogers, Mr C.A. Rowntree, Mr John Blundell, Mrs Blois-Brooke and the Imperial War Museum. Every effort has been made to trace all copyright holders, but some have been elusive. If any have been overlooked, the Publishers will be pleased to make the necessary acknowledgements at the first opportunity.

Maps

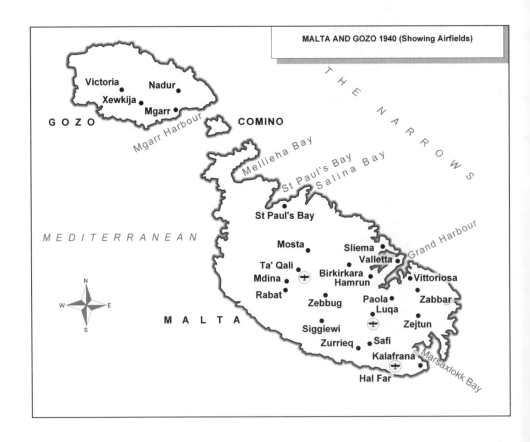

MALTA AND GOZO 1940 (Showing Airfields)

GOZO

Victoria
Nadur
Xewkija
Mgarr

Mgarr Harbour

COMINO

THE NARROWS

Mellieha Bay

St Paul's Bay

Salina Bay

St Paul's Bay

MEDITERRANEAN

Mosta

Sliema
Valletta

Grand Harbour

Ta' Qali
Mdina
Birkirkara
Hamrun
Vittoriosa

Rabat

Zebbug
Paola
Luqa
Zabbar

MALTA

Siggiewi
Zejtun

Zurrieq
Safi

Kalafrana
Marsaxlokk Bay

Hal Far

N
W E
S

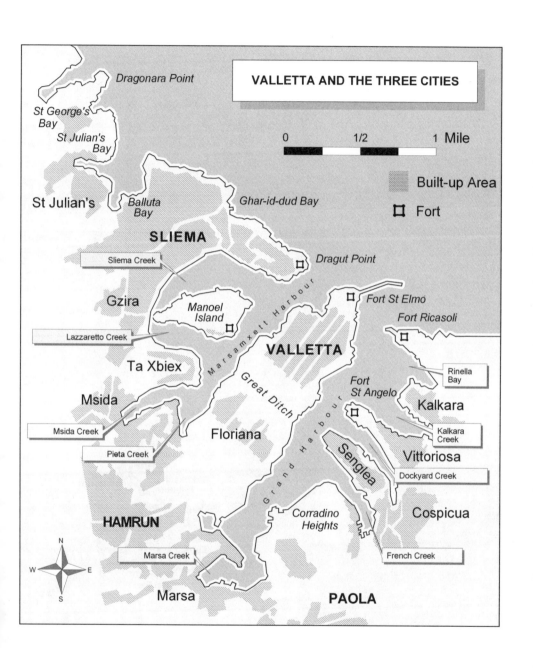

VALLETTA AND THE THREE CITIES

0   1/2   1 Mile

Built-up Area

Fort

Dragonara Point

St George's
Bay

St Julian's
Bay

St Julian's

Balluta
Bay

Ghar-id-dud Bay

SLIEMA

Sliema Creek

Dragut Point

Gzira

Manoel
Island

Fort St Elmo

Fort Ricasoli

Lazzaretto Creek

VALLETTA

Ta Xbiex

Rinella
Bay

Msida

Fort
St Angelo

Kalkara

Msida Creek

Floriana

Kalkara
Creek

Pieta Creek

Senglea

Vittoriosa

Dockyard Creek

HAMRUN

Corradino
Heights

Cospicua

Marsa Creek

French Creek

N

W   E

S

Marsa

PAOLA

Marsamxett Harbour

Great Ditch

Grand Harbour

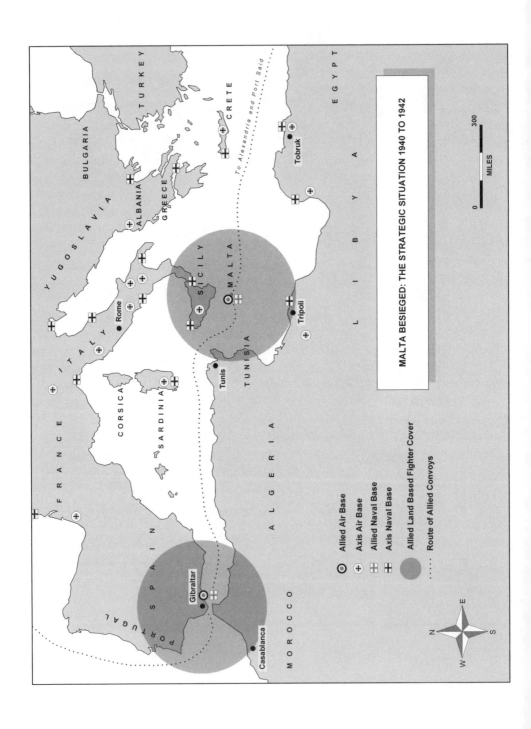

MALTA BESIEGED: THE STRATEGIC SITUATION 1940 TO 1942

Allied Air Base
Axis Air Base
Allied Naval Base
Axis Naval Base
Allied Land Based Fighter Cover
Route of Allied Convoys

FRANCE
SPAIN
PORTUGAL
Gibraltar
MOROCCO
Casablanca
ALGERIA
CORSICA
SARDINIA
TUNISIA
Tunis
ITALY
Rome
SICILY
MALTA
Tripoli
LIBYA
YUGOSLAVIA
ALBANIA
GREECE
BULGARIA
TURKEY
CRETE
To Alexandria and Port Said
EGYPT
Tobruk

0   300
MILES

N
W   E
S

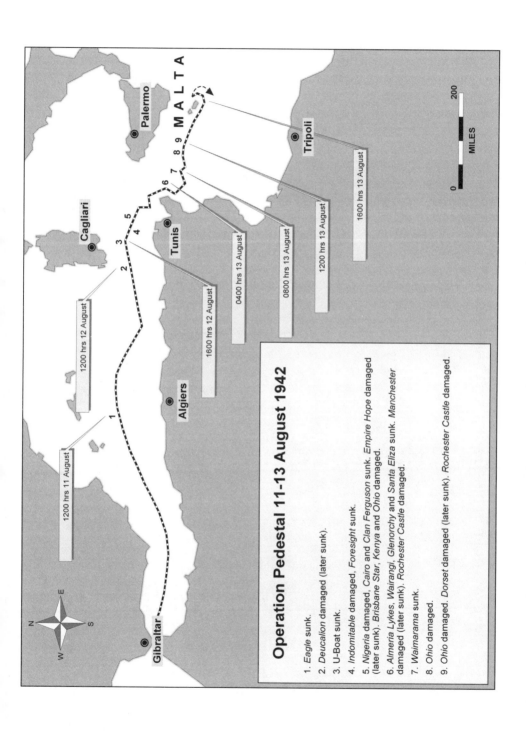

Operation Pedestal 11-13 August 1942

1. *Eagle* sunk.

2. *Deucalion* damaged (later sunk).

3. U-Boat sunk.

4. *Indomitable* damaged, *Foresight* sunk.

5. *Nigeria* damaged, *Cairo* and *Clan Ferguson* sunk. *Empire Hope* damaged (later sunk). *Brisbane Star*, *Kenya* and *Ohio* damaged.

6. *Almeria Lykes*, *Wairangi*, *Glenorchy* and *Santa Eliza* sunk. *Manchester* damaged (later sunk). *Rochester Castle* damaged.

7. *Waimarama* sunk.

8. *Ohio* damaged.

9. *Ohio* damaged. *Dorset* damaged (later sunk). *Rochester Castle* damaged.

MALTA'S ROLE IN DISRUPTING AXIS SHIPPING

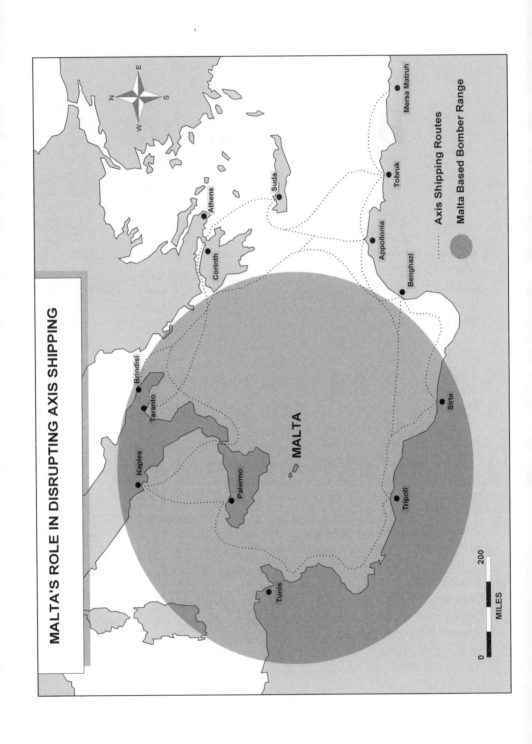

Axis Shipping Routes

Malta Based Bomber Range

Background

The Maltese archipelago consists of Malta and Gozo and three smaller islands, of which only one is inhabited. Malta itself is a small island 17 miles long and 9 miles across at its widest point. In 1939 its population was a quarter of million. What made Malta so important was its strategic position. It lies at the very crossroads of the Mediterranean. Sicily, the gateway to Italy, is just 60 miles to the north, while Libya – an Italian colony in 1939 – is 200 miles to the south. Gibraltar lies 1,000 miles to the west, and Egypt (and the Suez Canal) 1,000 miles to the east. Crucial to Malta's strategic importance were the two harbours at the capital of Valetta: the Grand Harbour, and Marsamxett Harbour, which with their creeks, provided the best naval base in the Central Mediterranean. The Grand Harbour was sufficiently deep to accommodate the most modern capital ships.

The history of Malta reflects the history of the Mediterranean. The island was controlled in turn by the Romans, the Arabs, the Normans and the Aragonese. In 1530, Charles V, the ruler of Spain and Holy Roman Emperor, gave Malta to the Knights Hospitallers of St John of Jerusalem. In May 1565 the Turks, under Suleiman the Magnificent, laid siege to Malta as a preliminary to invading Sicily. After an epic defence – often referred to in British propaganda during the much longer siege of the Second World War – the Turks withdrew on 8 September. The name of de Valette, Grand Master of the Knights of Malta who repulsed the invaders, lives on in the name of the modern capital city: Valletta.

In 1798 Malta was occupied by the French. Napoleon fully understood the strategic significance of the island, but he met with stiff resistance from the Maltese. Assisted by British naval and military units, the French forces were besieged at Valletta and ultimately

1

The Siege of Malta

forced to capitulate. In 1814 Malta became part of the British Empire: not by conquest, but on the request of its inhabitants. The British then began to construct a major naval base for their Mediterranean Fleet at Valetta, which by 1914 was the main employer on the island. In the First World War Malta served as a base for operations in the Middle East and as a major medical centre for the wounded. In this latter role the island became known as the 'nurse of the Mediterranean'.

In 1921 Malta was given 'home rule'. Subject to matters concerning foreign affairs and the naval base, the Maltese were free to run their own domestic affairs. Initially the Constitution worked well, but in the face of growing bitterness between the Constitutional and Nationalist Parties, it rapidly became unworkable and had to be suspended in 1930, before being finally abolished three years later. The consequence of these dissensions was that the Nationalist Party and the Catholic Church were branded 'anti-British' by the Constitutionalists. The Nationalists looked increasingly towards Rome for support, and the Mussolini Government did not hesitate to exploit the situation in Malta by appealing to pro Italian feeling.

When Italy invaded Ethiopia in October 1935, and Britain and France supported sanctions by the League of Nations against the Italian economy, relations with Italy rapidly deteriorated. Air raid practices were held in early 1936, and the authorities became aware of the need to win over public opinion. In a memorandum in 1935, which was drawn up by Malta Command, it was emphasized strongly that 'the maintenance of morale of the population is of the utmost importance in a fortress such as Malta where so many of the population are directly and many more indirectly connected with the Active Defence Services'.

The Ethiopian War ended in May 1936, but Anglo-Italian relations never recovered. Mussolini signed the Axis pact with Hitler in October and over the next three years steadily gravitated closer to Nazi Germany. The position of Malta thus became increasingly vulnerable to a potential Italian attack in the event of war. The Governor, Sir Charles Bonham-Carter, began to urge the authorities in London to build up the defences of the island, stressing that: 'it was unlikely that the fleet would be able to operate freely in the Central Mediterranean if Malta was held by the Italians'. In

Background

September 1936 the commanders of the three services based on the island optimistically agreed that: 'Malta can be made almost impregnable by the provision of adequate overhead cover and a sufficiently numerous and well equipped garrison.'

Over the next three years, as the international situation steadily became more menacing, some progress was made in building up Malta's defences. A new aerodrome was constructed at Ta' Qali in 1938, and plans were drawn up for creating a combined war headquarters, which would house key elements of both the Civil Government and the Armed Services. Steps were also taken to build up the local Maltese units. In early 1939 it was decided to recruit Maltese nurses and expand the Royal Malta Artillery and the King's Own Maltese Regiment (KOMR). But this was easier said than done. There was a considerable delay until the Treasury agreed to pay the Maltese units two-thirds the rate of the British units, and there was also an acute shortage of trained AA instructors and signal men.

The only help the Army could give was to promise not to withdraw any more instructors from Malta, which, as one staff officer in London remarked: 'although it may be of no positive assistance at least prevents your situation from becoming any worse'. In July 1939 the Committee of Imperial Defence agreed to supply Malta with forty-eight anti-aircraft guns, sixteen light anti-aircraft guns, twenty-four searchlights, and one fighter squadron: but it was not until February 1940 that the Treasury finally found the sums for them. Of crucial importance, however, was the installation of radar on the island in March 1939, although this only gave limited cover.

Equally important was the question of 'passive defence' or of safeguarding the lives of the population. Bonham-Carter had asked London for information about the construction of air raid shelters but it was not until the spring of 1939 that he received any assistance. In June, after viewing the alternatives, he urged the construction of deep bomb proof and underground shelters, capable of protecting about 140,000 people who lived in areas around the docks and naval base. The cheaper options of providing steel shelters for each household or strengthening basements were not practical, as there were very few houses in the urban areas that had basements or gardens. He hoped eventually to provide a comprehensive network so that nobody within Valetta and its suburbs would have to

3

The Siege of Malta

walk more than 150 yards to an entrance. Quite apart from the need to save life, he pointed out that: 'the defence would be gravely weakened if the population became affected by panic to such a degree that troops had to be used to establish control . . .' But to complete this scheme would take up to five years. Nevertheless the go-ahead was given to start work in Senglea, as this was where the majority of the dock workers and their families lived.

Considerable thought was also given to the food situation in Malta. At a London meeting of the 'Committee on the Services' Food Supplies in Time of War' in January 1938, an official at the Colonial Office put his finger on the potential vulnerability of Malta, if Italy were to declare war. In rather stilted 'officialese' he observed that 'because of its situation in the Mediterranean, the position of Malta might quite conceivably become a very unfortunate one. If normal sources of supplies were cut off, Malta might have to rely entirely on the UK, and there might be great difficulty in getting supplies there.' It was envisaged that at the start of the war a 'Malta convoy' would be dispatched to the islands, but the Navy was quite frank that thereafter it would be 'impossible to foresee how long would elapse before the next convoy could be got into Malta'. Nevertheless, Malta was requested to draw up a list of requirements based on the six-month rule.

The Governor authorized a detailed survey of Malta's food requirements by Borg Cardona, who had worked in food control in Malta during the Great War. Cardona highlighted some of the problems that were to become acute during 1942, although with hindsight he erred on the side of optimism:

- He pointed out that flour did not keep well in the Maltese climate, but was convinced it could be stored safely in 'the excellent storage facilities in the granaries constructed by the Knights'. The large flour mills were in the danger zone of the Grand Harbour area, but he assumed smaller ones could be used elsewhere on the island.
- He stressed that some 5,400 tons of kerosene were indispensable, 'as nearly all the cooking and much lighting and heating depends on this oil'. Its storage was particularly vulnerable. For only about half that amount was there moderately safe

4

Background

tankage. The balance would have to be pumped into the tanks at the Shell depot in Bizebugia, which, as Cardona ominously remarked, was 'an easy target for attacking aircraft'.

- He was confident that there would be sufficient local supplies of potatoes and onions.

The cost of building up a six-month reserve of essential food and fuels in Malta was way beyond the budget of the island and could only be authorized by the Committee of Imperial Defence and the Treasury.

One way of cutting down on the amount of food reserves needed was to evacuate the wives and children of all the British officials and servicemen. The Services favoured this solution and argued strongly that it would strengthen Malta, but both the Colonial Office and the Governor were conscious of how this might impact on the Maltese population. They feared the Maltese would see the evacuation as both alarmist and divisive. As one official at a meeting of the Overseas Defence Committee in March 1939 asked, would not the Maltese units be 'equally affected by the thought of their families being in danger of air bombardment'? However, while evacuation was not made compulsory, the War Office did encourage women with children and also those whose husbands had been moved away from Malta, to return to England. In April 1939 some seventy women and children arrived at Plymouth aboard the *Rawalpindi*.

Given the vulnerability of Malta to air attack, it is not surprising that in London both the War Office and the Air Ministry doubted whether Malta could be successfully defended. In January 1939 a joint War Office–Air Ministry memorandum argued that under heavy air attack it would be impossible to keep the naval dockyard open, even if defended by the maximum number of AA guns and search-lights. When the Committee of Imperial Defence met a month later, this view was echoed by both Sir Henry Tizard, the Government's scientific adviser, and the Army and Air Force representatives; but it was forcefully rejected by the naval representative, Captain Dankwerts, who according to the minutes:

wished to emphasize the fact that Malta, as a fleet base, was in existence, and could not be taken up and put down some-where else. It was absolutely essential to the maintenance of a

5

The Siege of Malta

fleet in the Mediterranean. The stronger the Italian Fleet became, the more necessary would be the facilities of Malta. Without it they could hardly hope to operate successfully against Italian communications. [Source: PRO WO32/2413]

The Navy again clashed with the Air Staff at another meeting of the Committee in July, when it was argued that no defensive plan would 'ensure the use of Malta for the Navy'. Lord Chatfield, the First Sea Lord, brusquely interrupted to stress that: 'nothing could be ensured in war, but if the defences of Malta were strong enough the Italian casualties [. . .] would be very disheartening to them.' Fortunately for Malta, both Sir John Simon, the Chancellor of the Exchequer, and the Foreign Minister, Lord Halifax, agreed that 'the political effect of deserting Malta would be disastrous.' The Committee of Imperial Defence subsequently accepted the need to defend Malta, although it was sparing in the forces it allocated.

In May 1939 any chance that Italy would remain neutral in the event of war with Germany appeared to be dashed by the 'Pact of Steel', which committed Italy to aid Germany if war broke out. Against the background of these ominous developments Colonel Burrows, the British Military Attaché in Rome, visited Malta for three days to report on its defences. When he returned he informed the British Ambassador in Rome that:

Considerable progress has now been made with the defences of the island. The regular infantry has been increased to four battalions with a total of about 2,000 men and there is a Maltese Territorial battalion of about 600 strong. The artillery has been increased and there are now in the island 42 A.A. guns, which it will soon be possible to man. Machine gun posts have been constructed at all possible landing places and are manned in emergency.

A barbed wire fence of limited obstructive power is being constructed along the Northern coast. The Air force consists of 4 obsolescent 'Swordfish' machines.

Every possible effort has undoubtedly been made with the means available and the spirit throughout the island is mag-nificent. [Source: PRO CO323/1657/91]

Background

Colonel Burrows and the Ambassador feared that at the very start of the war the Italians, in order to achieve an easy success for propaganda reasons, would launch an attack on Gozo with a force of 2,000–3,000 'desperate picked volunteers'. Burrows could think of 'no more tempting bait to the Italian Government desirous of obtaining a brilliant success to popularize the war with its unwilling people' and urged that it should be defended. The War Ministry accepted that the loss of Gozo would be a blow to British prestige, but argued that from a strategic point of view its occupation would not be a serious threat.

When Britain and the Empire declared war on Germany on 3 September 1939, the Governor informed the Maltese Council of Government that it was a 'struggle between two diametrically opposed conceptions of the state to each other. On the one side is the idea that the state should be the servants of its free citizens, on the other that all citizens should be the slaves of the state.' The irony of this was not missed by Dr Mizzi, the Nationalist leader, who pointed out that Malta itself had a semi-dictatorial regime. Privately the Governor conceded that the British had not handled the Maltese very well over the past 140 years and made them feel that: 'they were a people of an alien race, who happened to inhabit an island, the possession of which is essential to our sea power'. He agreed, however, that: 'all but a small minority are loyal, but the loyalty is in most cases due to the knowledge of which side their bread is buttered . . .'

In the winter of 1939/40 Italy remained neutral, and after the defeat of Poland, German troops remained passively on the Rhine. Malta was given a breather to strengthen her defences. Mussolini was not ready to declare war on Britain and France until it was clear that Germany was going to win. The Maltese Territorial Army was formed, and further increases in anti-aircraft guns, searchlights – even four squadrons of planes – were authorized in February 1940, although these had not reached Malta by the time Italy declared war in June. Indeed in April the Navy actually re-embarked the one fighter squadron on Malta, despite requests by the Air Ministry for it to stay!

In April 1940 the Governor, General Sir Bonham-Carter, suffered a heart attack and was invalided home. He was replaced, albeit at

The Siege of Malta

first as Acting Governor only, by Major General Sir William Dobbie, who had been GOC Malaya, 1935–39. Bonham-Carter, with his understanding and love of the Maltese, would undoubtedly have been an effective governor during the coming siege, but Dobbie was to be an inspired choice until his health also gave out, two years later. Dobbie was a paradoxical figure in ultra-Catholic Malta. He was a Plymouth Brother, whose religion denied the spiritual power of priests, yet during the siege his courage and unshakable conviction in final victory made him an effective leader, whom the Maltese could follow and respect. Admiral Cunningham called him an 'Ironside of a man'.

Dobbie arrived in Malta on 24 April, and the supreme military and civil control of the island was vested in him. Within a short time the international situation dramatically worsened. On 10 May Hitler invaded the Low Countries and by the end of the month the Dutch and Belgians had surrendered, the French were routed, and the British evacuating Dunkirk by any means they could. Italian intervention in the war was imminent.

Dobbie's first month was spent concentrating on both civil and military defence. The War Office, fearing an Italian parachute attack from Libya, instructed Dobbie to expand the second battalion of the KOMR into a specially trained anti-parachutist force. It realized the 'difficulties of training' but optimistically suggested 'enrolling local sportsmen with shot guns'. On the airstrip used for civilian planes, large numbers of barrels and derelict cars were placed, in order to deter Italian parachutists.

In light of the danger of parachute attack Dobbie also began rounding up 'enemy aliens' who might form a fifth column. Obvious candidates for internment were, for instance, a university professor who had been active in spreading Italian propaganda amongst his students, and a public works engineer who had good opportunities to look at military installations, and was busy distributing Axis badges, which would afford the wearer protection in the event of an Italian landing.

By the end of May Malta was holding its breath. The schools were shut and the children awarded an unexpected week's holiday. The teachers, however, were given courses on first aid and ARP work. In the first week of June all British married women with children who

Background

wanted to leave were given the chance to evacuate, but at least 500 English families opted to stay on the island.

Mussolini, fearful the Germans would win the war without his participation, rejected attempts by the British and French Governments to persuade him to remain neutral. On 10 June 1940 Italy declared war on Britain and France. Malta was now in the front line.

Campaign Chronicle

When the first air raid siren of the war sounded early on 11 June 1940, Malta's air defences consisted of four obsolescent Gloster Gladiators (with the fall of France the four squadrons of Hurricanes that had been promised back in February were now required to help defend Britain from imminent German invasion). The fact that even this meagre number of four planes existed was a stroke of luck, as they had been crated up in March 1940 for action in Norway, but had been inadvertently left behind by HMS *Glorious*. They enabled Air Commodore Maynard, in command of Malta's air defences, to form an operations flight of three with one plane in reserve. A month later he had to use all his formidable powers of persuasion to prevent the Navy from sweeping them away to Alexandria. In the absence of trained fighter pilots, seven men who had been flying sea planes, towing targets for AA guns to practise on, or doing office jobs volunteered to fly them . . .

June 1940: The Italian Blitz

Having declared war on the British Empire on the 10th, Italy launches a series of air strikes on Malta. For the next three weeks the island has only four outdated Gloster Gladiators to repel the raids. To escape the bombing, urban refugees flood into the villages causing chaos, overcrowding and potential health problems. The towns are left deserted and a prey to looters.

The four Gladiators were first scrambled for action at 6.49am on 11 June, but their inadequacies in comparison with the Italian aircraft became all too clear. They attempted to intercept a force of ten

June 1940: The Italian Blitz

Savoia-Marchetti 79 bombers, but it took them so long to gain sufficient height to attack, the Italians were able to drop their bombs on the Grand Harbour and form up to fly back to their bases in Sicily. But Flight Lieutenant Burges, who had been a former flying boat instructor, did manage to get the tail of one of the bombers in his sights and even pepper it with his .303 machine guns. The Savoia, however, soon escaped; and to make matters worse, one of the Gladiators was shot down and destroyed.

To overcome this problem Maynard realized the remaining Gladiators would have to scramble earlier. This meant their pilots would have to divide themselves into watches, and when on duty, they would have to sit strapped into their cockpits, despite the blistering Mediterranean sun, and take off as soon as the air raid alarm was sounded. This would save some sixty seconds and enable the Gladiators to climb an extra 1,000 feet. The six pilots thus took shifts of four hours on and four hours off during the daylight hours from 5am to 8pm.

On 11 June there were eight Italian raids in total. It was during the seventh that the first Italian plane was shot down. Flying Officer W.J. Woods described the event in his combat report:

> when climbing again to gain more height, I suddenly heard machine gun fire from behind me. I immediately went into a steep left-hand turn and saw a single-engine fighter diving and firing at me. For quite three minutes I circled as tightly as possible and got the enemy in my sight. I got in a good burst, full deflection shot, and he went down in a steep dive with black smoke pouring from his tail. I could not follow him down, but he appeared to go into the sea. [Source: *Air Battle of Malta*, p.11]

On 12 June two more enemy planes were shot down, but by 16 June the Italians began developing effective counter techniques. The bomber squadrons flew high, but one bomber in five would deliberately lag behind, acting as a decoy. When the Gladiators attempted to close on the straggler it would lose height, dropping beneath the Italian formation so the other bombers could train their movable guns at the pursuing fighters.

11

Campaign Chronicle

The Royal Italian Air Force (Regia Aeronautica)

In June 1940 the task of neutralizing Malta fell to 2 Squadra Aerea. A *Squadra Aerea* (Air fleet) consisted of two or more air divisions, which in their turn comprised each of at least two Air Brigades. These were subdivided into *Stormi* (wings), which usually were made up of two squadrons (*Grippi*). But the *Groupo* was the key operating unit and consisted of two *Squadrigle* (flights of nine aircraft), if these were multi-engine aircraft, and three, if they were single-engine. In December 1940 the Aeronautica della Sicilia (ASIC) assumed overall control of the campaign against Malta.

The Italian air offensive against Malta was badly hit by its poor supply organization and the slow rate in servicing aircraft. Fuel shortages, financial constraints and an alarmingly high accident rate combined to starve Italian pilots of the necessary training before combat. In 1940 a survey conducted for the Chief of the Italian Air Force Staff showed that only 30 per cent of the Regia Aeronautica's 5,000 or so pilots managed to reach a competent standard. Tactical communications were also poor. The two-way voice radio did not become standard equipment for fighters until 1943. Up to that date pilots still had, for the most part, to rely on hand signals.

In 1940 bombers were the dominant arm in the Regia Aeronautica and their pilots were trained to fight in close defensive formations, which would simultaneously release their bombs on the target. From combat experience in Spain

Until 28 June a force of three Gloster Gladiators, whom Flying Officer John Waters nicknamed 'Faith, Hope and Charity', were able at any one time to take off – despite crash landings, burst pistons and gun shot damage. To keep them flying the ground crews showed a genius for adaptability. Parts of a Navy Swordfish were grafted on to one Gladiator, while Blenheim bomber engines, discovered in the stores, were fitted into two others.

June 1940: The Italian Blitz

commanders had grasped the importance of fighter escorts and by late 1941 the Air Force was also beginning to practise the synchronization of level bombers, dive bombers and torpedo aircraft. Until they were provided with over 100 Junkers 87s from the autumn of 1941 onwards, the Italians also lacked suitable aircraft for dive bombing.

The Savoia-Marchetti SM79, which had first been tested in Spain, remained 'by default' – to quote Macgregor Knox, the expert on the Italian war economy – 'the Regia Aeronautica's most effective bomber.' Its successor, the SM84 had to be withdrawn from service in 1941–42.

The Air Force did develop monoplane prototypes in the period 1939–40, but at the beginning of the war the majority of fighters were still open cockpit biplane fighters. The mass production of the potentially excellent Reggiane Re 2000 was slowed by the Air Force Chief, Francesco Pricolo, because it needed high octane fuel for its most effective performance.

Fiat produced what one historian has called 'perhaps the worst monoplane fighter of the Second World War': the open cockpit G50. The ultimate solution was for Alpha Romeo and Fiat to produce under license the Daimler Benz engines, DB601 and DB605. This resulted in creating the 'adequately powered' MC202, but production was limited because the Alpha Romeo plant only obtained a mere seventy-four engines from Germany in 1941.

The defence of Malta rested upon a partnership of guns and fighters, but clearly the success of the fighters would be short-lived unless reinforcements could rapidly be sent. The Acting Governor, Sir William Dobbie, pressed London for a delivery of Hurricanes. The day after the first raid he telegraphed the War Office that the relative success of the raids showed: 'the importance of fighter aircraft. The four Gladiators here though successful in bringing one

13

plane down are too slow.' And he requested that a small force of five hurricanes, which were in Tunis en route for Egypt, should be sent to Malta instead. Two days later he returned to the subject and warned that: 'if fighters are not sent, it will in my opinion, eventually take the form of a dangerous mass demand for surrender, if we are not able to give reasonable protection to the population.' This message was further strengthened by Dobbie's Defence Secretary, who was: 'of the opinion that the next heavy raid will seriously affect public morale, unless a few fast fighters can be lent to us to break up bomber formations'. Finally the Commander-in-Chief of the Mediterranean Fleet, Sir Andrew Cunningham, gave his backing to these requests by stressing that it was: 'most important to sustain the morale of the Maltese population, who might have to resist attempts at invasion under conditions when immediate naval help was not possible'.

On 18 June the Air Ministry did dispatch a squadron of Hurricanes, but owing to bad weather and mechanical faults only four arrived, and two of those were ordered to fly on to Egypt. However, a further twelve were sent out to the island on 31 July. They were initially shipped to Gibraltar, where they were transferred to a carrier, HMS *Argus*. The convoy left Gibraltar on 31 July. The subsequent operation set a precedent for the way Malta would be supplied with fighter aircraft. The key to success was to create diversions, which would conceal from the Italians that the Hurricanes were to be flown to Malta. The first was an aerial attack from the *Ark Royal* on the Cagliari airfields in Sicily, intended to weaken the Italians' ability to attack the *Argus*, and the second was to lead the Italians to believe that operations were imminent in the northern part of the western basin of the Mediterranean by broadcasting a series of radio messages from a cruiser stationed off Minorca. On 2 August the Hurricanes flew off from the *Argus* and were able to reach Malta safely, except for one that crashed as it came down to land.

The first Italian raid of 11 June was made at 7.55am, just as people were setting off to work. According to Colonel Dixon, a British military doctor: 'The first bombs caused a sort of "primary shock" to the inhabitants, none of whom realized that war was like this.' Norah Goreing, daughter of the head groundsman of the Royal Naval foot-

June 1940: The Italian Blitz

ball pitch at Corrodino, was luckier than most, as her father had already constructed a deep shelter capable of housing the whole family. Later she remembered that when the sirens wailed:

> we awoke startled and frantically ran through the back door towards the shelter entrance. At that very moment the Italian bombers dropped the first salvo of bombs to ever hit the island. Five shattering explosions rocked the area as we dived for cover, leaving the glowing sunshine and headed into pitch blackness. [Source: Norah Jane Goreing: Memoir of a Head Groundsman's Daughter, IWM 92/30/1]

The main attack was directed at the dockyards: consequently it was Valetta and the towns around the waterfront that bore the brunt. The Government had made some progress in converting several tunnels under Valletta into air raid shelters, and a start had been made to tunnel under Senglea and Conspicua. Along the main roads slit trenches had been dug to provide protection for those who were caught out in the open. By 18 June about 19,000 people in Valetta and Floriana were living in tunnels and underground shelters. Elsewhere, where these facilities did not exist to the same extent, the population fled to the countryside. In the first few days about 100,000 refugees fled to what were optimistically called 'safe areas'. Kathleen Burke, a British teacher in Valetta, later described how: 'every car in the district was chartered, and motors, donkey carts, and lorries, piled high with furniture filled the narrow streets leaving for comparative safety, until even the milkman stopped coming round and not a shop remained open.'

Inevitably an exodus on this scale put a huge burden on the smaller towns and villages. Not all the evacuees had friends or family in the countryside. Many just turned up in the villages and were accommodated in schools, civic centres and churches. On 15 June the Government announced a system whereby each village appointed an official, who, in cooperation with the District Committee, the police, and the Special Constabulary, would be responsible for organizing the feeding and billeting of the evacuees. These officials were also to ensure that the sanitary system and water supply could adequately cope with the influx. A report from the small village of

Campaign Chronicle

Lija, which had to cope with a refugee population of 3,000, indicates what this work involved:

> preparing schools, rigging screen and partitions in public build-ings for families [. . .] making plank beds; collecting furniture, china and clothes [. . .] finding homes for refugees; persuading owners to accept them voluntarily; escorting lorries and buses to stricken areas [to bring over] evacuees and supplies; assisting in opening new shops; keeping order in houses without owners [. . .] organizing and controlling a soup kitchen, a maternity house, and a hospital-room for whooping cough cases. [Source: Joseph Micallef, *When Malta Stood Alone*]

The Church also played a key role in feeding the refugees by setting up 'Economical Kitchens', which were financed by weekly collections on Sunday from congregations throughout Malta, wherever there were gaps in the official provision.

In the meantime the towns were virtually deserted. One visitor to Vittoriosa observed that: 'I could not see anyone except starving cats and dogs.' Those who had not fled to the countryside had fled to the tunnels, which were packed with people living in the most unhy-gienic conditions. The empty shops and houses also attracted looters, and in the three months July–September the number of burglaries doubled compared to the previous year.

By the end of June there had been seventy-five air raids in which eighty civilians were killed and 180 injured. Except for the destruc-tion of the floating dock on 21 June, neither the naval facilities nor the aerodromes suffered serious damage. In the dockyards work had only been interrupted for comparatively short periods. The single most serious incident during the June attacks occurred on the 26th, when a bus full of passengers en route to Valletta was hit by an incendiary bomb at the Marsa Crossroads, resulting in twenty-eight deaths. On 7 July HMS *Olympus* was hit in No. 3 Dock and over 100 houses in the surrounding area demolished.

By late July the raids became less intense and the refugees began to return to the cities. As Kathleen Burke remarked: 'when the chief danger had abated, the overcrowding became more irritating and less tolerable than the off chance of being bombed.'

June 1940: The Italian Blitz

Instead of concentrating on Malta, Mussolini dissipated Italy's limited military and economic strength on a series of campaigns. Not only did Italian troops advance into the Sudan and British Somalia, but in early September they moved into Egypt and six weeks later attacked Greece through Albania. It was not surprising, therefore, that the overstretched Italian Air Force could launch only a series of sporadic raids on Malta in August and September. Dobbie reported on 20 August that there had been a 'considerable relaxation from bombing and a return to normality', but he had already warned London not to crow too loudly over this as:

> minimization of the effect from Italian raids on Malta may only produce intensification of these attacks. At present there is reason to suppose that they have deliberately not attacked so fiercely as they would have the world believe, and it is suggested that the Italian dream of intensive damage done should be allowed to continue in view of our meagre defences. [Source: PRO WO 106/3062]

That the Italians could still launch effective raids was shown by their attack on two of Malta's three aerodromes on the same day, 20 August. This resulted in the damaging of a number of Blenheims, which were passing through en route to Egypt. In early September the Italians began using German Ju 87s, and in raids on 15 and 17 September, for example, delayed action bombs were dropped on Hal Far airfield. However, in the first half of October there was only one air raid. Altogether, in the five months from July to early January 1941, there were 146 alerts and only five civilians were killed and fourteen injured.

The lull in the bombing gave Dobbie the chance to strengthen Malta's defences and build up her reserves of supplies. The Coordinating Committee of Supplies (COSUP) was set up in Malta, which handed a formidable series of shopping lists to the Colonial Office. These demanded everything from lubricating oil, condensed milk, rubber teats for babies' bottles, wheat, sera and vaccine to 3,000 tons of cement, 150 tons of ½-inch bar steel and 10,000 tons of coal. Initially the aim was to build up a six-month reserve, but then, when the Cabinet decided Malta should become an offensive

Campaign Chronicle

base by April 1941, this was raised to eight months. The Colonial Office and the Crown Agents (Government procurement agents) performed miracles in meeting Malta's demands. The cement was found in Durban, the coal in India and the wheat in Australia.

But getting the materials to Malta was a considerable challenge. The bulk had first to go to Alexandria, where the Malta shipping Committee took responsibility for dispatch to Valletta. Some light cargoes – like the babies' teats and medical equipment – could go by air, but as Admiral Cunningham had stipulated that the lowest speed he could accept for any ship was 12 ½ knots, the problem of finding suitable shipping became, to quote one official at the Colonial Office, 'a little involved'. In the end, space was found on the fast merchantmen *Clan Ferguson* and *Clan Macaulay*.

In London it seemed that the Maltese authorities were at times taking a somewhat cavalier attitude towards the problems of shipping. They turned down Egyptian wheat in favour of Australian, but when J.B. Williams, the official dealing with Malta at the Colonial Office, dared suggest they should take what they could get, the Colonial Minister, Lord Lloyd, argued that: 'the risk of impairing morale of the people of Malta if they were forced to eat the type of bread to which they were not accustomed was too great.' The same desire to maintain morale also dictated the decision to import a few goods such as books and a limited quantity of foodstuffs, which were not classified as essentials.

At the end of September Dobbie wrote to the Colonial Secretary:

Now that you have been presented for the first time with a complete picture of Malta's requirements for the next six months and shipping space needed, I am not surprised that you are impressed by totals. Accumulation of so many large orders for early dispatch is of course mainly intended to equip Malta in matter of supplies for the part assigned us by Chiefs of Staff primarily to make Malta available as a base for the Mediterranean Fleet by April 1941. To do this we must be fully prepared by that date for retaliation which may cut us off from further supplies for a considerable time . . . [Source: PRO CO852/346]

June 1940: The Italian Blitz

The Battles of Calabria and Taranto, July and November 1940

On 8 July a flying boat from Malta spotted the Italian Fleet 200 miles east of Malta and heading southwards. It was attempting to deny the Central Mediterranean to the British Fleet, so that a vital convoy could reach Libya. Despite the superiority of the Italian Fleet, Admiral Cunningham decided to risk an engagement. On 9 July the *Orion* and *Neptune* sighted the Italian cruisers and destroyers. In the subsequent action the Italian flagship, the *Cesare*, was damaged and the fleet withdrew to the safety of its home base. Cunningham drew the conclusion that the Royal Navy would have no trouble in dominating the Mediterranean from Alexandria, and that the fleet could survive attack from the air. Events, however, were to show how inaccurate this assumption was to be, once the Luftwaffe moved into the Mediterranean.

Ironically the next major British success against the Italians showed the crucial importance of air power. The *Illustrious*, a modern aircraft carrier, had been ordered out to join the Mediterranean Fleet. Since he had failed to force a sea battle on the Italians, Cunningham hoped to launch an airborne attack on their fleet as it lay at anchor in Taranto harbour. Long-range fuel tanks were fitted to the torpedo-carrying Swordfish aircraft on the *Illustrious*. The attack, which took place on the night of 11 November, was a complete surprise, as the Italians assumed the presence of the British Fleet off the Greek island of Cephalonia was intended to protect the passage of convoy MW-4 to Malta. Two battleships were damaged, another, the *Cavour*, put permanently out of action, and a cruiser and two destroyers were also hit. Indeed, half the Italian Fleet was put out of action for several months at the cost of two downed British planes. As Ernle Bradford has written: 'the aircraft carrier showed itself to be the most potent weapon at sea, and the battleship joined the long ranks of ships that had once dominated the oceans and whose day was over'.

Campaign Chronicle

The dispatch of regular convoys to Malta was made easier by Cunningham's naval successes at Calabria and Taranto. By the autumn and early winter of 1941 convoys were managing to reach Malta fairly easily:

- On 2 September two cargo ships arrived at Valetta.
- On 7 October another store convoy reached the island.
- In November, Convoy MB-8 delivered 2,150 troops, MW-3, five store ships and MW-4 a further four.

July 1940: The State of Maltese Morale

The Italian raids have failed to break Maltese morale, but there is fear in Government circles that a prolonged siege and further heavy bombing could cause the population to lose faith in Britain's ability to defend the island. In the worst scenario the authorities fear large scale civil unrest and demands for surrender.

Although Italian air raids progressively diminished from July onwards, the state of civilian morale much exercised the Government and the service chiefs in Malta. The Vice Admiral, for instance, in his report on the raid of 7 July, stressed the 'morale of the population was still good but lack of adequate defences by air and AA guns is causing this to deteriorate'. Three weeks later Dobbie was more optimistic, but emphasized that keeping up civil morale was 'about the most important factor in the security of this fortress'. And this meant presenting visible evidence that Malta's air defences were being strengthened and Italian raiders were being shot down. Once the Maltese overcame their initial fear of the raids, they took great delight in watching the aerial combat, and according to one witness:

All over the country there were cheers and excited cries, as the people saw the enemy meet their just fate at the hands of our gallant pilots, and our English and Maltese anti-aircraft gunners. In one fishing village there was a demonstration, boys and girls carrying trophies from destroyed planes . . . [Source Micallef, *When Malta Stood Alone*, p. 46]

July 1940: The State of Maltese Morale

The Government attempted to bolster the morale of the civil population in two ways: through propaganda from London and, what was probably in the final analysis far more important, accelerating the construction of air raid shelters. At top level, Prime Minister Winston Churchill and the King sent messages of encouragement. Churchill, with considerable accuracy as it turned out, predicted in June that: 'you will make the defence glorious in British military history, and also in the history of Malta itself.'

On a more practical level the British people were asked to contribute to the Malta Relief Fund, which had been set up in August to help with looking after refugees. One Maltese doctor residing in London was somewhat critical of the contribution from the British Empire. By the end of September only £800 (over £20,000 in modern terms) had been raised, while the Maltese themselves had contributed £8,000 to the Spitfire Fund. However, contributions did pick up in October. Lord Nuffield gave £1,000, the Viceroy of India War Purposes Fund, 15,000 *rupees* and the King £100, although his cheque was mislaid in a safe in the Colonial Office for three months!

The BBC also began a series of broadcasts to Malta on 10 August. These were read by Maltese speakers in London. The BBC was anxious they should not be used just as a means for countering enemy propaganda. Officials from the Malta Information Service provided raw material for the first broadcast in late July, which did not hide that there had initially been a massive exodus from the towns, but stressed that the Maltese, like the British, were clinging to liberty 'with the tenacity of a bulldog'. To emphasize the *sang froid* of the Maltese it told an amusing anecdote about a dog sniffing an unexploded bomb: 'He treated the bomb to the age old canine gesture of contempt, which was indeed an appropriate salute to this message of goodwill . . .'

On 7 September Lord Lloyd gave the broadcast, drawing parallels between Malta's current siege by the Italians and the Great Siege by the Turks, which was raised on 8 September 1665. And the Colonial Office was also anxious to ensure that coverage of Malta was provided by the popular press. One official minuted: 'The idea is to get the "popular" press – *Daily Mail*, *Express*, *Evening News* and *Standard*, which write staccato leaders, to arrange if possible for a ten-line laudatory paragraph in a leader from time to time.'

Campaign Chronicle

On the island, the Malta Information Service sent out a series of news bulletins in both English and Maltese. There were also radio broadcasts, and loud speakers were set up at appropriate points across the island. The Colonial Government described them as: 'an essential and invaluable channel for the dissemination of information, the guidance of public opinion and behaviour, maintenance of morale and issue of air raid warnings'. Contact with the local press was also utilized, journalists being fed relevant information and encouraged to use it. Meanwhile there were talks about the need to cut down on imports, the *Real Italy* and the *Voice of America* etc.

But crucial to maintaining the morale of the Maltese was the construction of adequate shelters. On 19 September the War Office anxiously asked the Colonial Office about the progress being made with the 'main deep shelter scheme'. It stressed that: 'the security of Malta depended to a considerable extent on the morale of the local population, and unless adequate shelters are provided [. . .] the effect on the Maltese may be such as to endanger the efforts of the defending troops.'

Given that it would have taken another four years to have completed the original deep shelter programme, the Maltese authorities concentrated on a crash programme of blast and splinter proof shelters (except where rock formation made it possible to tunnel rapidly). These took the form of trenches or cellars covered with slabs of reinforced concrete and rubble, which were designed to resist anything but a direct hit from a heavy bomb. With the help of the Navy, which made available members of its civil engineering department, over 50,000 people were provided with shelters by December 1940, and it was expected that by the following April the whole population of Malta (though not Gozo) would be provided for.

August–December 1940: Malta's Strategic Role

Governor Dobbie and the Chiefs of Staff consider Malta's strategic role. They fear that any attempt to conduct offensive operations could provoke an Italian attack.

The fall of France had increased Malta's strategic importance in the Mediterranean. It was the only British base between Gibraltar and

August–December 1940: Malta's Strategic Role

Alexandria, and was also an important aircraft staging post between Britain and the Middle East. The problem, however, was that if Malta tried to play an offensive role in the war she might provoke an attack that would eliminate her usefulness as a base. General Dobbie put this argument in a nutshell, when he wrote to the CIGS, General Sir John Dill, on 21 August 1940:

> It is not that I am anxious about the safety of Malta. Please God we can, and will hold it against anything the Italians do – but I want to ensure that its usefulness to Imperial defence will not be impaired. Of course, it is a dangerous argument to Imperial defence to assume that if we don't hit the other fellow, he won't hit us. But it is probably true that if we do hit him and become a nuisance he will try and abate the nuisance by hitting us.' [Source PRO WO 216/114]

When, on Churchill's recommendation, the Chiefs of Staff considered the potential role of Malta two days later, they stressed that Germany was Britain's principal enemy, so bombers could not be spared for Malta. They echoed Dobbie's sentiments about hazarding Malta's role as an important staging post for a half-baked offensive role as a bomber base, stressing that: 'under present conditions [. . .] this plan must be deferred until the forces on the Middle East have been considerably strengthened. Our greatest present handicap is the absence of sea communications.'

But Admiral Cunningham pressed strongly for making Malta usable as a base for light naval forces and submarines by April 1941. In this he had Churchill's complete backing. On 12 July Churchill had already made it clear that Malta should be made a secure base for the Fleet. The Chiefs of Staff accordingly agreed to build up the anti-aircraft defences by April 1941 and increase the fighter strength to four squadrons as soon as possible.

Over the next few months the Maltese garrison received considerable reinforcements. The Admiralty supplied two cruisers and four destroyers. The number of Glenn Martins was increased to twelve, while a battery of field guns, as well as a few tanks were sent out. In November the 4th Battalion of the Royal West Kents disembarked with gun crews and RAF ground personnel, which were immediately sent to strengthen the defences of Luqa and Ta' Qali aerodromes. The military infrastructure was also improved by the addition of an extra aerodrome and underground installations for aviation fuel and bombs.

But supplying Hurricanes was a more difficult task. On 15 November a squadron flew off the *Argus* as far westward from Malta as possible to avoid Italian naval units, but only four reached the island as the others had run out of petrol. It was not until early January that the *Essex* arrived with twelve crated Hurricanes and the added bonus of 3,000 tons of seed potatoes.

By November Dobbie was much more optimistic about Malta's strategic role. On 9 November he wrote to the CIGS that he was 'very happy about things in general' and was all in favour 'of hitting them from Malta and anywhere else we can'. Four days later his wishes were realized when the Italian Fleet at anchor in Taranto was attacked by aircraft from the *Illustrious* (see textbox on page 19).

For the Armed Forces the main threat to morale lay in the extremely irregular delivery of post. Between May and September, for instance, an average of just two letters for each serviceman had been received. And it was particularly irritating that trade circulars and advertisements made up a considerable part of the few deliveries that reached the island! In June and July the troops had been kept busy clearing bomb damage and preparing defensive positions, but once the bombing eased they were employed in general training aimed at defending the island from a possible invasion. According to General Dobbie: 'The defence plan, if the enemy effect lodgement, must be active and not passive. It is not so much a question of holding on in certain positions as of rapid and ruthless counter-attack to dislodge the enemy whenever and wherever he gains a footing.'

Diseases such as sand fly fever, scabies, and dysentery (known as 'Malta Dog') were common, but effectively treated by the military hospital at Imtarfa. In October a system of 24-hour leave passes was introduced, where soldiers could spend a night in one of the official service clubs.

An unforeseen advantage of the war was that it gave the Government a chance to grasp various political nettles it had been avoiding in peace time. In a memorandum to the Colonial Office Dobbie high-lighted educational reform and tackling unemployment as important long term goals. He felt that after the war unemployment could be managed through a mixture of emigration and birth control. He also wanted to break the grip of the Catholic Church (perceived as pro Italian) on education by encouraging high school students to go to the more English orientated St Edward's College rather than St Aloysius, which the Colonial Secretary regarded as a nest of 'pernicious pro Italian propaganda'. The hope was that boys at St Edward's, would, as Lord Lloyd observed, be taught the 'elementary duties of loyalty and patriotism to the Empire of which they are a part'.

Another problem was the continued uncertainty about who would replace the elderly Archbishop of Malta, Caruana. The British candidate was Father Zarb, but the fear was that the pro Italian

The Political Background

In 1930 Lord Strickland – former Prime Minister of Malta, leader of the Constitutionalists, and owner of the influential paper the *Times of Malta* (his daughter Mabel acted as editor) – enraged the Maltese Catholic Church by making a series of provocative criticisms. In response Archbishop Caruana forbade any Maltese from voting for Strickland's party. Those that did vote were barred from taking Communion. The tension between the Constitutional and Nationalist Parties became so acute that the Government had to intervene and suspend the Constitution. Strickland's supporters accused the Church of being pro Italian, Mabel telling the Colonial Secretary in July 1943 that: 'the spiritual penalties under which the island suffered, 1930–32 were far greater than the subsequent Italian bombing.'

The British Government was far from hostile to the Catholic Church, but there were pro Italian priests and pro Italians in the Nationalist Party. Consequently London was anxious that when Caruana died, the next Archbishop should be an anglophile.

Campaign Chronicle

Bishop of Gozo might be appointed instead. Although the Cardinal Secretary in Rome had been reassuring, there lurked the anxiety, in the words of Colonial Secretary Lord Lloyd that: 'if anything suddenly happened to Caruana, we might be faced with some awkward *fait accompli.*'

Dobbie's dealings with the two main Maltese political parties, the Nationalists and Constitutionalists, was made difficult by the devious manoeuvres of the latter's leader, the semi-senile Lord Strickland – aided by daughter Mabel. Dobbie complained to London that: 'they are causing me far more worry than the Italians and Germans together. They seem prepared to throw a spanner into my works if I don't govern the country exactly in the way they like.' Strickland did not hesitate to brand any political opponent in the Nationalist Party, including the Chief Justice, as a 'Quisling', urging Dobbie to have them interned. The Governor was only too aware that the Constitutionalists were loyalists, but he told the Colonial Secretary on 28 July 1940:

> I naturally am incessantly on the look-out for subversive elements, and any whom I think may be a danger to the fortress, I intern without hesitation. I think I have erred on the side of safety and have interned too many rather than too few, but I am not going to use my position to play his party game for him. [Source PRO CO 967/87]

Inevitably the combination of defence problems and domestic politics created a heavy burden on the Government. Minimizing the stress on individual officials was, for the medium term, as important a precaution for the security of the island as building up its defences. As Dobbie perceptively remarked at the end of September: 'the evils arising out of the present strain and failure to relieve that strain will sooner or later create a really dangerous situation directly affecting the security of the fortress.' He was particularly worried about the workload of the Lieutenant Governor, Sir Edward Jackson, and managed to persuade London to send a Home Office Official to assist him: 'he must be a first rate official,' demanded Dobbie, 'Any other would in the circumstances be worse that useless.'

January 1941: The German Blitz

By December 1940 life, in many ways, seemed to be getting back to normal, although the increased garrison and the continued existence of refugee centres did not allow the island to forget there was a war on. All the cinemas and bars had reopened, as well as the Royal Opera House. And on 20 December the feeling of normality was enhanced by the visit of Admiral Cunningham's Flagship, the *Warspite*, and its destroyer escort to the Grand Harbour. Cunningham was given a rapturous welcome, recording in his memoirs that: 'as we moved in with our band playing and guard paraded, the Barracas, and other points of vantage were black with wildly cheering Maltese. Our reception was touchingly overwhelming.' To add to the festive feeling the north wind, gusting down from the Sicilian mountain ranges, had even brought a few flurries of snow.

On Christmas Eve Midnight Mass was held in the afternoon as the lighting of candles was forbidden. On the following day a series of parties – organized by air raid wardens, special constables and British service personnel – were thrown for the children of Malta. But crucial to this feeling of relaxation was the fact that the Italians kept their aircraft grounded between 21–28 December. For Christmas Day the report from HQ RAF Malta to the Air Ministry in London recorded: 'No air operations undertaken. Clouds 1,500 feet and rain. No enemy activity over Malta today.'

January 1941: The German Blitz

*The Germans intervene with devastating consequences
for Malta and British sea power in the Mediterranean.
Britain's largest and most modern aircraft carrier,
HMS* Illustrious, *is badly damaged by a heavy German
air attack on the 9th – the so-called 'Illustrious blitz'.*

By the end of December 1940 Italy was on the defensive in both Greece and North Africa. The Greeks had thrown the Italians back into Albania, while the British had not only advanced into Libya, but were also dispatching reinforcements to Greece. The combination of these Allied successes persuaded Hitler that German forces would have to intervene decisively in the Mediterranean theatre if his future plans for an attack on the USSR were not to be endangered from the south. On 11 January he issued Directive No. 22, which

Campaign Chronicle

The German Air Force (Luftwaffe)

At the beginning of the war all operational flying units were divided into *Luftflotten* (Air Fleets). Each *Luftflotte* comprised a balanced, self-contained force with its own fighter, bomber, reconnaissance and other units. The prime aim of the Luftwaffe was to enhance mobility and free up planes to concentrate, when required, at a particular point on the front. Flying units were therefore freed of their administrative and supply organizations by the *Luftgauen* (Air zones or regions), and each had the necessary administrative and supply personnel. The parallel operational organization to a *Luftgau* was a *Fliegerkorps*, which usually operated between 300 and 750 bombers, fighters, transport planes, etc.

The key fighter unit in the Luftwaffe was *die Rotte* (literally cell). This consisted of just two planes: one acted as *Rottenführer* or leader, while the other was his 'wing-man' or *Katchmareck*. Each pilot covered his partner's blind spot behind and below. In a dog fight or combat, the *Katchmareck* would watch his leader's tail. Two *Rotten* formed a flight (*Schwarm*), while three made up a *Staffel* (squadron).

As Dr Alfred Price in *The Luftwaffe Databook* (Greenhill Books, London, and Stackpole Books, Pennsylvania, 1997) has pointed out, there are three factors to consider in assessing how effective a combat formation is: 'first is the ability of the formation to manoeuvre while maintaining cohesion; secondly, the ability of the pilots to cover each others' blind spots and thus prevent a

ordered preparations for the dispatch of German troops to Tripoli and Greece. Crucial to the success of these operations was the elimination of British sea power in the Mediterranean and the destruction of Fortress Malta. Already in December, as Malta was celebrating the Christmas lull, Fliegerkorps X (Air Corps), composed of over 200 bombers and Messerschmitt fighter escorts, moved down to bases in Sicily, where its Stuka dive bombers began practising on mock up models of HMS *Illustrious*.

January 1941: The German Blitz

surprise attack, and thirdly the ease with which an aircraft in the formation could receive support if it came under attack'. Judged by these criteria the Luftwaffe was highly effective. In a *Schwarm* or a *Rotte*, the fighters of which flew about 200 yards apart, the Germans developed the cross over turn, in which each plane turned as tightly as it was able, and exchanged positions in the formation. Surprise attacks were made less likely by the fighters' ability to protect each other's blind areas and the cross turn rapidly dealt with an attack from behind.

Broadly speaking German fighters tried to 'bounce' their opponents out of the sky if at all possible. If they themselves were 'bounced', and unable to carry out a cross over turn, they could go into a high-speed dive. This was made possible by the direct injection fuel system, which had been fitted to their Daimler Benz or BMW engines. Another option was the *Abschwung* (sharp bank), which was to quote Price: 'a half roll pulled through into a steep dive at full throttle'.

The German bombers most frequently used over Malta were the single-engine Ju 87 (the celebrated 'Stuka' dive bomber) and the twin-engine Ju 88. The aircraft flew in a three-plane *Ketten* (arrow or V formation). For accuracy, dive bombers dived into the wind to hit their targets. If the designated target was fairly small, the leading aircraft initiated the dive with the others following. For larger targets, however – such as the dockyards and harbours of Malta – the V formation was maintained for the attack.

The opportunity of attacking the real aircraft carrier presented itself with the launching of Operation *Excess*, which involved the passage of two supply convoys through the Mediterranean to Crete, Piraeus and Malta, one sailing from Gibraltar under Admiral Somerville and the other from Alexandria with the *Illustrious* and Admiral Cunningham's flagship, the *Valiant*. Initially the operation went well. On 9 January the two convoys met north-west of Malta, Somerville's escorts turned round to sail back to Gibraltar, while

Campaign Chronicle

Cunningham prepared to escort the Malta-bound merchantmen to Valletta. The following day at 12.20pm the *Illustrious* had little difficulty in repelling an attack by two Italian Savoia bombers, but then, five minutes later, she was overwhelmed by a swarm of forty Ju 88s and Stukas, followed closely by a second wave of Ju 88s. The Germans skilfully and bravely carried home their attack and achieved what has been described by Ian Cameron as 'one of the great flying achievements of the war'.

Within six and a half minutes the *Illustrious* was hit six times, and 126 of her crew were killed and ninety-one wounded. The carrier itself was badly mauled, her steering gear out of operation and massive fires raging in her holds, but she was still afloat and her engines worked. Her only option was to sail to Malta for emergency repairs. By a judicious combination of jamming the rudder and varying the revolutions of her main engines, she managed to limp into the Grand Harbour at nine o'clock that evening.

The *Illustrious* was berthed at the Parlatorio Wharf, French Creek. She was in fact little more than a steaming hulk stinking of oil, cordite, and human blood and guts. To quote historian Ernle Bradford: 'So the very face of war was seen in the heart of the island.' The wounded, many of whom were suffering from severe burns, were rushed off to Imtarfa hospital by a fleet of ambulances, while the dead were put on a mine sweeper and buried at sea so hastily that their bodies were not sufficiently weighted down and they were later to resurface and wash up against the southern cliffs of the island.

The damage was assessed that very night by the engineers, who came to the conclusion that as her engines were functioning, the *Illustrious* could, after some emergency repairs, sail to Alexandria. Early the following day dock workers swarmed onboard and work began. The key question, of course, was how long would they have before the next raid? For five vital days the Luftwaffe left the *Illustrious* in peace, except for a small-scale and ineffective attack on the 13th. This hiatus gave the island a brief opportunity to prepare for the coming onslaught, and enabled Brigadier Sadler – just arrived from organizing the anti-aircraft defences of Dover – hastily to plan a 'box barrage' aimed at defending the dockyard and the Luqa and Hal Far airfields. The principal behind a box barrage was that during

January 1941: The German Blitz

an air raid the AA guns would put up a curtain or 'box' of exploding shells through which the attacking planes would have to fly if they were to reach their target. The dockyard box was only finalized a mere one hour and ten minutes before the first great German attack came on the 16th.

The day before, RAF Headquarters had noticed that: 'one enemy aircraft reported as a Heinkel 111 or Ju 88 approached from north and circled over Grand Harbour at 21,000 feet. Engaged by AA, no bombs dropped. Mission presumably reconnaissance.' Then at 1.55pm on 16 January over seventy German planes attacked. The first wave consisted of Ju 88s escorted by Italian CR 42s, while the second and larger one was of Ju 87 dive bombers.

As they had done a few days earlier, the Germans again showed remarkable courage and skill as they dived through the intense artillery barrage put up by Sadler's 'box'. The *Illustrious* was the main target, but it was hit only once, on the quarter deck, sustaining minor damage. Meanwhile, widespread collateral damage was inflicted on Valletta and neighbouring Vittoriosa, Senglea and Conspicua (the so-called 'Three Cities'). The carrier's survival owed something to the box barrage and the small number of intrepid British fighters, but equally importantly, French Creek also enjoyed considerable natural protection from the Corrodino Heights on the one side and Senglea on the other. It was also obscured by enormous clouds of dust and smoke, thrown up by bomb damage to the adjacent buildings. E.T. Hedley, a dockyard worker recalled how:

> the entire island rocked to the shock of battle. The thud of the heavy stuff, which the Junkers were dropping, the roar of the bombs as they exploded, and the rumbling crash of masonry as Senglea and Vittoriosa caught the weight of the enemy's attack.
>
> The Stukas followed their squadron leaders in the screaming plunge into the inferno that was raging over the creek. Some of them did not emerge. The defenders were just as tough as the attackers. It required nerve to stick to your guns with those thousand-pounders thudding and bursting around you with those screaming furies diving over you. [Source Micallef, *When Malta Stood Alone*, p. 62]

Campaign Chronicle

The shelters near the dockyards shook with the blast of the bombs and as one witness recalled: 'women and men alike, screaming prayers, were toppled on each other [. . .] children began to cry, while outside the shattering noise continued [. . .] It looked as if the world had come to an end.'

The experience was equally terrifying for Norah Goreing. Her father's shelter had been enlarged and opened as an underground pub. When the '*Illustrious* blitz' started, she remembered:

> There was a crowd of sailors sitting around us from the *Illustrious*. Their suffering was reflected by their drawn and tired faces. They were unshaven and looked grey in the face and worried by their recent experiences [. . .] and as the pandemonium went on, speech was impossible. So one of the *Illustrious*' sailors decided that it was time for a sing-song, he stood up and began singing First World War songs as loud as he could, then his mates and everyone in the shelter joined in and sang as loud as they could to try to drown out the din. As they towered over us, they looked enormous with beer glasses in their clenched fists. The ground shuddered as more bombs dropped nearby, particles of limestone dust fell from the ceiling covering their blue serge uniforms. [Source IWM Goreing 92/30/1]

At least these sailors were in the relative safety of a shelter. Lieutenant Commander Blois-Brooke, on receiving orders to rejoin his ship, the *Imperial*, had to leave a cave shelter in the middle of an air raid and make a mad run for it:

> I could hear splinters whistling around me and soon became confused by the blinding flashes and deafening explosions. After about 100 yards I took shelter behind a static water tank. This was a mistake. It was difficult to get myself going again – but somehow I did, and finally arrived onboard puffing like a grampus and sweating like a pig.

On the opposite side of the creek from the *Illustrious* a heavy bomb hit the *Essex* in the engine room with a loss of thirty-eight merchant

January 1941: The German Blitz

seamen. If the bulkheads had not held, 4,000 tons of ammunition and torpedoes would have exploded and destroyed everything in the creek.

Two days later about eighty Ju 87s and Ju 88s, covered by fighters, attacked the Hal Far and Luqa airfields in two waves, in an attempt to destroy the RAF's fighter planes before returning to finish off the *Illustrious*. As the Combined Service report revealed, considerable damage was done:

> About 40 1000 lb bombs scored on each target. Luqa 2 hangers completely destroyed, 2 badly damaged. 1 Wellington burnt out. 1 Glenn Martin badly damaged. All remaining aircraft slightly damaged by shrapnel. Aerodrome unserviceable. Buildings destroyed are Signal Section, 1 barrack block and decontamination centre, other Offices and NAAFI damaged. Electric power, telephone communication and water cut off. 2 airmen killed in shallow trench, 5 others slightly injured. Hal Fal 1 hanger direct hit. Hurricane inside write off. 3 swordfish burnt out, 1 other total loss. Several aircraft minor damage, many craters but NW–SW strip serviceable. Officers' mess destroyed. Telephone communications completely cut, water mains hit. [Source: PRO WO106/3065]

The RAF could only muster a fraction of the German force: five Hurricanes and three Fulmers, but between them they managed to shoot down six enemy planes, while AA fire accounted for three more.

There was one more attack on the *Illustrious* on the 19th, but again the ship escaped serious damage. The Luftwaffe, however, lost some eighteen planes. Inevitably this rate of loss forced the *Fliegerkorps* to pause and regroup before launching any more attacks. It was during this lull that the *Illustrious* was able to slip out of harbour. She made such good speed at over 20 knots that her escorting destroyers missed their rendezvous with her. She underwent further temporary repairs at Alexandria and then had a complete refit in Norfolk, Virginia.

Campaign Chronicle

February 1941: The Luftwaffe Ascendant

While Rommel arrives at Tripoli to take charge of Axis forces in the Western Desert, the Luftwaffe continues to attack Malta – almost every day there are fighter sweeps and heavy attacks on the airfields.

After a lull in late January and early February, enemy air activity began to increase from 5 February onwards. The Germans began dropping parachute mines in Marsa Muscetto and the Grand Harbour, which often missed and landed on the Three Cities and the dockyard areas. From the middle of February the Germans stepped up their efforts to achieve air superiority. On 16 February, for instance, two formations of Messerschmitts, which outclassed the Hurricane Mark Is, flew over Malta. HQ (Malta) RAF reported that: 'On spotting the Hurricanes they split up, one formation climbing above the other, the other dropping below the Hurricanes . . .' Nevertheless, the Hurricanes managed to account for one of the intruders, which was shot down. For the next three months the Luftwaffe continued to wage a war of attrition against the RAF and its airfields. On 18 March Dobbie described the pattern of the German attacks to the War Office:

> attacks on aerodromes generally built up in intensity over period of about a fortnight, firstly very thorough daily recon-naissance followed by one or two attacks by two or three high flying bombers protected by fighters, Ju 88s and Me 109s, culminating in intensive combined dive bombing and low level bombing attack by up to 100 planes. These attacks always protected by some 25 Me 109s and 110s, flying 15000–2000 feet, are carried out by 20–30 Ju 87s, who dive from 7000–8000 feet right down to 100 feet of their target, whilst 20–30 Dorniers and Heinkels low level bomb from 8000–5000 feet. [Source: PRO WO106 3065/18/3]

At Luqa aerodrome on 27 February a squadron of Wellingtons was virtually destroyed, and a week later sixty bombers attacked Hal Fal aerodrome. A few days later the remaining Wellingtons, together with the Sunderlands, had to be withdrawn from the island.

February 1941: The Luftwaffe Ascendant

Gradually the RAF was beginning to lose supremacy of the air. The Axis had lost almost 100 over Malta since June 1940 and the RAF only about sixteen. But the Axis powers had plenty of reserves, while the RAF had virtually none.

Crucial, therefore, to the defence of Malta was the regular dispatch of fighter replacements. Fighter aircraft were being sent to Egypt from the Cape either cased or by carrier, where they were fitted with long range tanks and flown into Malta when opportunities presented themselves. In the first two weeks of March a squadron of Mark II Hurricanes managed to make it from Egypt. A fortnight later, on 3 April, another twelve flew off the *Ark Royal* 400 miles west of Malta. At the end of the month the SS *Parracombe*, disguised to look like a neutral ship, tried to slip through to Malta with another twenty-one Hurricanes, but she sank after hitting a mine off Cape Bon. Nevertheless, further consignments of Hurricanes, which were flown off carriers, did continue to reach Malta, bringing the total number of serviceable fighters up to forty by early May.

April witnessed the heaviest and most sustained period of bombing the island had yet suffered. During the night of Easter Sunday, 13/14 April HQ Malta reported that: 'About 30 aircraft some identified as Ju 87s and Ju 88s came over in three waves' – bombs rained down with varying intensity for the following hour and a half. Another large scale raid on the dockyard occurred on the 23rd. But the impact of these attacks was dwarfed by the night raid of 29/30 April, when according to a Government report: 'a large number of enemy aircraft came over and dropped mines and bombs. This was followed by a second wave which dropped more bombs.' There was damage throughout the island but Valletta fared the worst. Norah Goreing later recalled that: 'Between raids we emerged from the shelter like frightened animals . . .'

Despite its reinforcements, the RAF performed disappointingly in May. Air Vice Marshal Maynard reckoned this was due to the in-experience of new pilots, and the fact that the Mark I Hurricanes were not the equal of the Messerschmitts. But of course, fatigue also played a role. The Air Ministry sent out five experienced flight leaders and replaced the pilots of No. 261 Squadron, who were sent off on leave to Egypt. A second fighter squadron was formed (No. 185) and the control organization was improved. Fighter Command

Campaign Chronicle

sent out a staff of control officers under an experienced wing commander, plus some modern communication sets facilitating fighter control from the ground. In the meantime, Fliegerkorps X was being transferred to Greece and North Africa to replace units earmarked for Germany's invasion of the USSR.

The '*Illustrious* blitz', as we have seen, was on a far larger scale that anything Malta had up to that date experienced: buildings were destroyed and people killed or trapped for hours in ruins in Valletta and the Three Cities. At Vittoriosa, for instance, all but one of the thirty-three people who had been sheltering in the sacristy of the parish church of St Lawrence were killed before they could be rescued, and the one survivor, Lorenza Pisani, died later in hospital. ARP units, demolition squads and servicemen all rushed to the scene to help; and Dr L. Mifsud Bonnici, the Medical Officer of the Cottonera Centre, organized a first aid post in a tunnel at Marina, Senglea. But it was clear that help was needed on a much larger scale, and the *Times of Malta* complained that: 'it was noticeable that demolishing squads and rescue parties were insufficient to cope with the work and that the removal of debris was being conducted in the normal, slow, peacetime manner by Government workers [. . .] Volunteers were turned down in large numbers the evening before.'

On Saturday 18 January the Government at last brought in the Armed Forces. Units of the Royal Engineers, the King's Own Malta Regiment and the Royal Malta Artillery moved to help with recovering bodies. Lieutenant Commander Blois-Brooke, was attached to the Malta Artillery, while his ship, HMS *Imperial* was being repaired. He remembered how the work was:

> both sad and disgusting. Sad because there were inevitably relatives waiting about for mothers, fathers, sons, etc. [. . .] and all the time these relatives would keep up a sort of a dirge in Maltese, nothing would stop this frightful noise, not even a request to keep quiet because we wanted to listen for a cry or some noise which might lead us in the right direction. And disgusting because we came across a body that might have been dead for a long time. [Source: IWM/Blois-Brooke/95/5/1]

February 1941: The Luftwaffe Ascendant

The Government also decided to organize the evacuation of the Three Cities. Units of the Royal West Kents, the Devons and the Dorsets were put in charge. They commandeered all the trucks and buses that could be found, and by Monday the Three Cities were again ghost towns populated by abandoned pets. By the end of January only 4,000 out of 12,953 inhabitants remained, and looting again became a problem.

Compared to June 1940 the reception of the refugees by the villagers in the countryside fleeing the bombing was much more reserved. Families were more reluctant to be burdened with strangers, who took up scarce space and stayed for an indefinite period. Initially the Government asked those who were ready to offer billets to 'place on or near their front door the sign of a Maltese Cross in paper, paint or chalk or whatever medium is in hand, as an emblem of hospitality [. . .] Those with large houses should take in several people.' This was only partially successful and in March there were still many refugees living in schools and the crypts of churches. Consequently local Protection Officers resorted to compulsory billeting in houses where the residents were occupying only 25 per cent of the premises. Small 'nuclear' families were even asked to 'amalgamate and give up one house instead of having strangers billeted upon them'. The communal Feeding Service was revived and mobile canteens offered food at low prices at the various reception centres. These were subsidized by the Malta Relief Fund and the Help the Homeless Committee. And, as it was still in the middle of the damp, chilly Maltese winter, appeals were made for clothing and blankets.

Fleeing the Three Cities did not of course guarantee immunity from bombing. Luqa and Hal Fal were particularly dangerous areas, but the whole island, town and country alike, was vulnerable to attacks by the German dive bombers. Crucial to the preservation of morale was the speediest implementation of the shelter programme and the introduction of a compensation scheme for damage of property and life and limb as a result of the air raids.

Understandably the population was becoming increasingly sceptical of concrete shelters and was demanding the provision of the far safer rock shelters. The *Times of Malta* rapidly made this a major campaigning issue, and in his 4 February broadcast Dobbie stressed that the Government was 'straining every nerve' to provide them. But this was not an easy task: there was a shortage of tools, miners and quarry workers. Initially, after the *Illustrious* 'blitz', 400 miners from Gozo fled home and refused to return until their own villages had been provided with rock shelters. To ensure that the public tunnelling programme was maintained the Government had to introduce labour conscription and import a large number of picks and compressors from Egypt. By April over 1,200 miners were employed on shelter construction and Government statistics showed that on 1 May, out of a total population of 241,659, some 139,000 had access to rock shelters.

Nevertheless the tempo of construction was disappointing, and the *Times of Malta* was full of examples of how the miners were procrastinating. One reason for this was that tunnel workers could earn considerable sums excavating private shelters. Consequently, as the *Times of Malta* observed, they tended to 'consider the time with the Government as a time of rest and start the day's work with private employers'. The *Times* attempted to persuade the Government to put the miners on piece rates, but it stuck to its policy of daily payments, although it placed the miners under the supervision of twelve British NCOs.

In an attempt to accelerate shelter construction there were calls for volunteers by the Church, District Committees and leading members of the community. In Pieta, a small number of young women, who were assisted by their husbands and their children, began to dig a rock shelter for their families as early as 26 January. A month later one of them described their labours:

> We commenced to dig our own shelter [. . .] The larger part of the workers were SCs [Special Constables], Wardens and members of the MVDF [Malta Volunteer Defence Force], but little girls and boys helped in clearing the unearthed rubbish [. . .]. The climax of the afternoon came when the sirens wailed, but work continued without a single thought to the enemy above us. As the sun sank lower into the horizon, we dropped our picks and shovels and trudged off to our beds with blisters on our fingers, and weariness in our bones, but with the full conviction that what we started to do will prove useful towards

February 1941: The Luftwaffe Ascendant

the maintenance of the security of our folk at home. [Source Joseph Micallef, *When Malta Stood Alone*, p. 87]

In June there were still thousands of people outside Valletta and the Three Cities who had no shelters at all. However, in November, Dobbie was able to announce at the opening of the third session of the Council of Government that: 'by the end of this month there will be space available either in public rock shelters for people or in private shelters, whether of rock or concrete, for the whole population of Malta . . .' and that work was continuing on Gozo, where some fifty out of 175 shelters were completed.

The other important measure to be taken was the introduction of a Government-backed scheme to compensate for loss of property and personal injury. The initial protracted debate between the Colonial Office and Valletta on what form such a scheme should take prompted Churchill to minute on 21 January: 'Surely they should be allowed to come into our own scheme on nearly the same terms as our own people, and in retrospective effect.' In due course details of the UK legislation were sent out as a model. In discussions on the Executive Council the Government was persuaded to agree to making limited 'retrospective payments [. . .] in respect of serious or prolonged disablement'. In the end the Personal Injuries Bill was approved by the Council of the Government in August. In essence it permitted pensions for widows, children's allowances and temporary grants to be made at 55 per cent of the UK rate. A month later the Government reported that the scheme was working well, but inevitably anomalies did emerge. In one case the Government was unsure whether it could grant a pension to adult sisters who had been maintained by their brothers. In another case, as one official minuted: 'as a piece of light relief, the committee received an application from a gentleman who had gone half blind from the shock of hearing over the Rediffusion that Italy had entered the war. He claimed this to be a war legacy, but regrets had to be expressed.'

In the aftermath of the raids the Government also had to organize the demolition of damaged houses, the clearance of sites and the salvage of property left inside. Up to 30 April some 2,000 houses were severely damaged. Then there was the problem of removing debris from bomb sites and blocked roads. It was calculated that all this would take at least six months' work. Given the shortage of petrol and motor transport, the rubble was shifted in carts or even manhandled 'to the nearest available square or other suitable place', where it was then sorted, and what was still usable taken by the Army and RAF for their defensive construction work.

The Government only had four demolition squads and had to ask London for the necessary money to double that number. Sir Edward Jackson, the Deputy Governor, informed the Colonial Office that: 'if we do not get our 8 squads we shall fall further and further behind the damage. It is very bad for morale that a lot of property, including daily necessities, should remain under destroyed buildings, and it is also very uneconomical from every point of view to leave these buildings uncleared.'

April 1941: Rationing Introduced

By January 1941 Malta had seven months of stocks, but the arrival of the Luftwaffe in January prevented the delivery of any further supplies until March. In early February 1941 the Government at last decided to introduce a single coherent rationing scheme to replace the local schemes run by the RPOs (Regional Protection Officers). Three new offices were set up for the Coordination of Supplies, the Control of Food and Commerce and the Food Distribution Office. All heads of families had to register at their local Protection Office and declare the number of children younger than eight years old. Ration cards were then distributed on Monday 7 April. Initially only sugar, matches, soap and coffee were rationed, but in August the list was extended to lard, margarine and edible oil. Kerosene, which was used by the Maltese for both cooking and heating, was rationed and distributed to individual families once a week by small horse-drawn tankers.

Owing to the shortage of convoys unrationed goods became increasingly scarce and could only be obtained on the black market at very high prices. Tinned sardines and tuna fish, which were the staple diet of the working classes, became a luxury, while fresh meat was hard to find. According to reports in the press it was a daily occurrence 'to see people fighting, pushing and shouting themselves hoarse all day long in order to buy their meat and other commodities'.

As the Mediterranean Fleet was greatly overstretched by the War

April 1941: Rationing Introduced

The Greek and Cretan Campaigns, 1940–41

Italy invaded Greece on 28 October 1940. Initially Churchill was able to send only fifteen aircraft and some anti-aircraft batteries. The Greeks were not only able to drive the Italians out of Greece but to invade Albania. In March 1941 60,000 British troops were sent from Egypt to Greece. In response, a month later (6 April), the Germans began occupying Yugoslavia and simultaneously bombed the Greek port of Piraeus. Six Allied merchantmen with military cargoes were destroyed and the whole harbour was wrecked when the *Clan Fraser*, which was carrying ammunition, was hit and blew up. By the 19th British troops were retreating to the southern Greek ports and evacuation to Crete started on the 24th.

Anxious to defeat the British before turning to Russia, Hitler decided on seizing Crete by airborne troops. The attack was launched on 20 May, but thanks to successful decrypting of German signals by *Ultra*, the Germans were only able to take Crete after heavy casualties. And yet Churchill's decision to try to hold Crete caused severe naval and air losses, which weakened the British position in the Mediterranean. On 28 May evacuation was ordered. In Malta fears grew that the Germans would launch another airborne invasion, and that Fliegerkorps X would return to Sicily expressly for this purpose: but the withdrawal of Fliegerkorps VIII to the north, in preparation for the attack on Russia, ensured that Fliegerkorps X would have to be based in North Africa, Greece and Crete.

Cabinet's decision to send British troops and equipment to help the Greeks in January 1941, and Malta itself was under intense attack from the Luftwaffe, Admiral Cunningham was unable to send a convoy until late March. Ten days before it sailed he wrote to Admiral Pound:

> I am really seriously concerned about Malta. I am running a convoy there in about ten days time, but with their defences in

the present state I am quite expecting some ships to be damaged. The Grand Harbour and the creeks are also being mined whenever the enemy cares to come. This is a gloomy picture, but someone is misinforming the Chiefs of Staff about the real state of affairs out here. We must have large numbers of fighters rushed out to us if we are to make any headway, and indeed they are needed to save what may be a serious setback. [Source: Quoted in James Holland, *Fortress Malta*, p. 129]

Convoy MW-6 consisted of three ships from Haifa and one from Alexandria with coal, cement and a mixed cargo of foodstuffs. It sailed close to Crete so that the Fleet Air Arm forces based at Maleme could give it protection. It was sighted, but was saved from attack by low clouds, and arrived in Malta on 23 March. Once in harbour the *Perthshire* received a direct hit in the forehold, and the *City of Lincoln* was struck on the bridge by another small bomb. This time most of the supplies could be saved, but the attack did highlight the vulnerability of merchant shipping in the Grand Harbour and the need to get vessels unloaded as quickly as possible. Dobbie was able to breathe a sigh of relief and tell the Colonial Secretary that: 'all is well. We are glad to get the last convoy in . . .' but he added: 'I wish we did not have to bother the Navy to run these convoys for us – but I am afraid we cannot help it.'

Temporarily at least, Cunningham was able to reassert British control of the Mediterranean, when he ambushed the Italian Fleet on the night of 27/28 March off Cape Matapan, sinking a heavy cruiser, two light cruisers and two destroyers.

In early May the British took a considerable risk with Operation *Tiger*, which involved sending a convoy of fast tank-carrying ships to Egypt, whilst simultaneously escorting two smaller convoys to Malta from the east. On the 5th the *Breconshire* and two slow tankers sailed from Alexandria and again managed to berth safely in the Grand Harbour, but the *Empire Song* hit a mine and sank. On 10 May the Vice Admiral, at Malta, reported that the Italians had mined the area from Cape Bon to Maritino Island, leaving only a small channel swept, which he hoped to discover by sending a submarine to shadow northbound Italian ships from Libya. For the present he was of the opinion that: 'any further attempts to run a convoy from west to east would be most hazardous'.

May 1941: Allied Reverses in the Mediterranean

Will Malta be invaded? For the first four months of 1941 this seemed unlikely as the Navy still controlled the Mediterranean, but after the fall of Crete on 28 May, Dobbie fears Malta could be next on Hitler's list.

On 22 January 1941 Dobbie received cables from the War Office telling of reports circulating in Rome that 30,000 German troops were in Sicily. At first Dobbie was confident that the existing garrison was sufficient in Malta 'to ensure that any attempt contemplated must be really a big one and so may be a deterrent'. Two weeks later, however, he conceded that invasion was 'a contingency that had to be faced'. In view of the *'Illustrious* blitz' and the subsequent raids, Dobbie was again anxious about the reaction of the population and feared the Army might be faced with the task of controlling the population whilst simultaneously fighting the Germans. He consequently asked the War Office to send at least one more battalion, which, he added, should bring their own bicycles with them as a means of transport around the island.

By early June the strategic situation was transformed by the British withdrawal from Greece, the fall of Crete, and the heavy naval losses connected with these catastrophes. On 22 May German dive bombers had sunk the *Fiji*, the *Gloucester* and four destroyers, and had badly damaged the battleship *Valiant*. A week later Rommel captured the Halfaya Pass and stood at the gateway to Egypt. Unsurprisingly Dobbie wired London on 5 June with a new and more urgent appreciation of the threat to Malta:

> The recent operations in Crete and elsewhere have again changed the defence situation of Malta. When my original appreciation was made it was considered certain that the Fleet would intervene at Malta within a few days. It seems possible now that Malta might have to stand the full weight of a German airborne attack probably supported by a subsidiary

seaborne attack for a much longer period. Previously the loss of local air superiority has been reluctantly accepted but the seriousness of such a situation has now been brought home to us . . .' [Source: PRO WO 106/3067]

He was now convinced that the Axis forces would attempt invasion because it was the only base from which their communications with Libya could be effectively attacked. The 'outstanding lessons' from the Crete fiasco demanded that Malta should have: Sufficient fighter aircraft in operation; the capacity to deal with parachutists before they received reinforcements and established themselves; the means of preventing an aerodrome or landing strip falling into enemy hands; sufficient forces to repel a seaborne attack, which might be synchronized with an airborne attack.

Dobbie's shopping list therefore requested more men, planes and AA guns. He wanted two more infantry battalions with carriers, motor cycles and bicycles, another squadron of fighters, more field and anti-tank guns, and the dispatch of the 2,577 personnel in Egypt, of whom 1,000 were gunners. These had already been earmarked for Malta and were simply waiting for shipping space and the sailing of a convoy.

Despite the transfer of German forces to Eastern Europe in preparation for the invasion of the USSR, the fear of a parachute drop on Malta continued to persist. A remark by 'Lord Haw Haw' in one of his propaganda programmes from Berlin that yellow flaps were being worn on gas respirators in Malta alarmed the Governor, as this was the recognition signal in case German parachutists were disguised in British uniform. Troops stationed around the three aerodromes practised defending them from imaginary parachute attacks and counter-attacking if they were seized by the Germans.

June 1941: Malta Reinforced

Success or failure in the Western Desert hinges on the effective disruption of Axis communications between the ports of southern Italy and Tripoli from Malta. Consequently it is vital to keep the island reinforced.

June 1941: Malta Reinforced

In view of Malta's strategic importance as a base for attacking Axis communications the War Office agreed to reinforce the Malta garrison with two battalions of infantry, one heavy and one light anti-aircraft regiment, thirty field guns with the necessary teams and more RAF pilots and technicians. Since Fliegerkorps X had been moved from Sicily to Crete and Cyrenaica, it was decided to risk sending a convoy from Gibraltar to Malta, which was code-named Operation *Substance*. It consisted of six merchant ships and one troop ship, the *Leinster*. As the Italians had five battleships and ten cruisers ready to sail, the convoy's escort was strengthened with units from the Home Fleet, the battleship *Nelson* and the cruisers, *Edinburgh*, *Manchester* and *Arethusa*. The plan was to escort the convoy from Gibraltar to the Skerki channel, where it would then turn back to Gibraltar, leaving a much smaller force – Force X under Admiral Syfret – to carry on to Malta. Meanwhile the fleet from Alexandria would create a diversion, leading the Italians to assume it was heading for Tobruk. Submarines were to patrol the Tyrrhenian Sea and the RAF from Malta and Gibraltar would provide reconnaissance and anti-submarine patrols.

But the convoy did not get off to a good start. It left on 20 July, but the *Leinster* ran aground and its personnel had to be taken back to Gibraltar. Meanwhile, the NAAFI in Malta had carelessly sent in commercial code, rather than through official channels, a signal to London with details of purchases to be shipped in Operation *Substance*. The Admiralty in London feared that this 'gross laxity had probably compromised this most important operation'. Fortunately, however, these signals had not been picked up and the Italian surface fleet made no attempt to attack. But on the morning of 23 July, when the convoy was south of Sardinia, the Regia Aeronautica launched a well synchronized attack by six torpedo bombers and nine high level bombers, which hit the *Manchester* and the destroyer *Fearless*. Colonel Westropp, who was on the *Manchester* with his battalion, later described the action in his memoirs:

> Directly after we had been struck, the watertight doors in the aft part of the ship were ordered to be closed, thus saving the ship but condemning any man who was alive on the lower deck and on the stern side of the doors to be drowned [. . .]

Campaign Chronicle

> During the action the men were crammed together in the dark with the ship heaving over following a great explosion and the thought in their minds that there was no chance of escape if she went down. [Source: IWM/ Westropp 75/25/1]

The *Manchester* was ordered to return to Gibraltar. Westropp himself, after attempting to reassure his men, settled down to read *Barchester Towers*: 'thus distracting my mind with the machinations of the formidable Mrs Proudie and the odious Mr Slope . . .'

When the rest of the convoy sailed through the Skerki Channel the Italians launched a further attack by submarines and motor torpedo boats, hitting but not sinking the *Sydney Star*. The troops she was carrying, and some of her crew, were immediately transferred to the *Nestor* and she was able to sail on alone, reaching Malta on 24 July, a few hours before the main convoy, which had taken a longer route.

The day before (23 July) the *Breconshire* and six empty ships managed to slip out of the Grand Harbour. They split into groups according to size and kept close to the Tunisian and Algerian coastline. If the French stopped them and attempted to take them into their North African ports, they were to be scuttled. Although they were attacked by Italian aircraft, they managed to return to Gibraltar safely by the 28th. The troops and RAF personnel, who had been left at Gibraltar or had returned on the stricken *Manchester*, were then embarked on warships and in Operation *Style* speedily dispatched to Malta, which they reached on 2 August. While en route the *Hermione* sighted in the moonlight and rammed an Italian submarine. Colonel Westropp observed that she 'cut into the submarine, rolled her over and swept over the top at 28 knots; none of the crew were rescued.'

On 28 July Dobbie congratulated the Admiralty on the success of *Substance* and remarked that: 'the cargoes show that exceptional efforts had been made to meet our requirements.' As well as bringing essential commodities, *Substance* and *Style* boosted the size of the garrison to 22,000 men, brought the number of heavy anti-aircraft guns up to the original target of 112, and light guns up to 118, which was a considerable advance on the previous target of sixty.

July 1941: *Operazione C3*

On the night of the 25th, under cover of an air raid, the Italians launch a brave but foolhardy attack on the Grand Harbour.

Although the Italians had failed to destroy the *Substance* convoy at sea, they did make a brave but doomed attempt to destroy the six merchantmen in harbour. Under cover of a synchronized air raid, a submarine was to breach a narrow boat passage into the Grand Harbour. This was temporarily closed by an anti-torpedo net, which was suspended from the viaduct spanning the gap over the entrance to the Grand Harbour. Then MTBs were to pass through rapidly and sink the merchant ships in the Grand Harbour, while a two-man submarine was to the attack the submarine base at Fort Manoel. The force consisted of: a large, fast torpedo boat carrier, the *Diana*, which transported eight one-man EMBs (Italian Explosive Motorboats); two torpedo boats, each towing a two-man submarine with a detachable explosive bow; a motorboat to rescue the crews of these two craft once they had found their targets; and a larger motorboat to take all the personnel back after the attack.

But the operation went disastrously wrong. The parent ship *Diana* was picked up by Malta radar at 8.55pm, just south of Sicily and approaching Malta. By 11pm this had been tracked to within 14 miles of Malta. All the coastal guns were manned and an air raid siren was sounded. Soon motorboat engines could be heard, but they were too far out to sea to be picked out by search lights. The air raid, which was supposed to mask the sound of an attack from the sea lasted from 12.13 to 14.43am. One minute after the all-clear an explosion was heard at the foot of St Elmo, and then a second explosion brought down the breakwater viaduct that ran over the entrance to the Grand Harbour. The search lights were immediately turned on and fire was opened on the Italian raiding force at a range of 1,000–3,000 yards. In a few minutes, to quote the official War Office notes: 'fire was stopped as there appeared to be nothing left to fire at . . .' At 5.30am fire reopened when two objects thought to have been wrecks were seen to move. In a few minutes both sank and exploded under the water. The motorboats that had covered the two EMBs and the two-man submarines were shot up by Hurricanes before they could escape. In the dogfight with the Italian Macchis, which had been belatedly scrambled to protect the Italian motorboats, three were shot down at the cost of one Hurricane. The RAF pilot managed to bail out and get into his dinghy. As the sun came up he spotted a torpedo boat bobbing in the waves. He rowed over to find that the crew had been killed, but managed to hoist a white flag. He was later spotted and rescued by a Fleet Air Arm Swordfish. Ella Warren, who worked in the Naval signals office, remembered that: 'among things saved from the boat was a little mascot white furry dog with a red bow: what girl gave it to what boy? We named him "Bruno-Bianco" and he swung on a cord above my typewriter and his little black eyes gave nothing away.'

The submarine that was intended to attack the base at Manoel Island ran aground and its crew was captured swimming ashore in St George's Bay, which was more than 2 miles from the Grand Harbour. It is likely the crew had been confused by the bays and inlets of the Maltese coastline and had completely missed their target area.

August 1941: Malta – the Key to the Mediterranean

Submarine and bombers based on Malta are able to interrupt Axis supply lines to Tripoli and harry the Sicilian and southern Italian coasts.

Once Fliegerkorps X had transferred its attentions to North Africa and Crete, Malta increasingly became an important base for air, submarine and surface attacks on Axis shipping, harbours and aerodromes. These were greatly assisted by the cracking of the German cyphering machine (*Enigma*) and the Italian naval cyphers by the Intelligence Service called *Ultra*, based in Bletchley Park, Bedfordshire. Malta played a key role in 'listening' to enemy cypher messages and sending them to Bletchley for decoding. They were then transmitted to the Special Liaison Unit at Malta for the attention of the Commanders-in-Chief in the Mediterranean. Nevertheless a large part of intelligence gathering was still dependent on reconnaissance carried out from submarines and aircraft.

August 1941: Malta – the Key to the Mediterranean

Captain G.W.G. Simpson

The submarine base was set up by Commander G.W.G Simpson, or 'Shrimp', in early 1941. Simpson was an eccentric, but in many ways inspiring commander. He was the only naval officer to keep pigs, which provided his men with fresh meat. Neither did he stand on ceremony; he believed in encouragement rather than iron discipline. When he debriefed his crews, he would rarely censure a captain for a missed opportunity; instead he quietly pointed out the errors made and had the gift of inspiring rather than intimidating. Captain Norman, who commanded the *Upright* remembered one case of potential mutiny, which could have ended in a court martial, being quietly defused in a highly unorthodox manner. A rating turned up for duty completely drunk:

> He was singing, shouting and swearing that he was not going to go out on any f*****g patrol, etc., etc. This was reported to Shrimp, who asked the lower deck to be cleared and everybody to be mustered on the jetty. This done, Shrimp came down and had the rating brought up supported, before him. He asked, 'Are you going to join the sub?' 'I'm not going on any f*****g sub.' Shrimp ordered that a heavy line should be brought up and tied round the rating. This done, he said, throw him in the water, followed a short while later by 'pull him out.' Again he was brought dripping before Shrimp. 'Are you going?' 'I'm not going . . .' 'Throw him in.' I think he was thrown in four times before his last appearance before Shrimp, when he gave his reply, 'Of course, Sir, thank you.' And that was all that was ever said.' [Source: IWM/ E.D. Norman 99/75/1]

In early 1941 a base for small manoeuvrable submarines was set up on Manoel Island in Marsamuscetto Creek. These were ideal for the shallow waters around Cape Bon, Benghazi and Tripoli. Acting with the torpedo-equipped Swordfish planes, they were able to inflict significant damage on the convoy route to Tripoli. In February the *Upright* sank the Italian cruiser, *Armando Diaz* off the Kerenna Bank, and a month later the *Utmost* torpedoed and sank an Italian transport and two German supply ships, the *Heraklia* and the *Ruhr*.

On 13 August the Air Ministry informed the AOC Malta that: 'it is extremely important that all possible steps are taken to curtail further enemy communications with North Africa.' Until the return of the Luftwaffe at the end of December, this is exactly what happened. By October over 60 per cent of the supplies being sent to Rommel were sunk. The daily secret cypher messages to Whitehall from Malta revealed a successful and apparently uninterrupted tale of reconnaissance and successful action. To take just one report on 8 August, for example:

> Three Blenheims sighted convoy 6 M/Vs (Motor Vessels) and 6 DRs. Did not attack owing strong fighter escort. Night 6/7 August 7 Swordfish torpedo attacked convoy off Lampedusa. Five torpedoes released. Number of hits not known but M/V 8000 tons and second of 6000 tons sunk, confirmed by all aircraft; only 4 M/Vs and 6 DRs seen later by Blenheims A.M, 7/8 [. . .] Blenheims bombed same convoy attacked by Swordfish now consisting of 4 M/Vs, 6 DRs at 0545 hours 80 miles E.S.E. of Kerkeneh. Two direct hits with 500lb bombs on an 8000 ton M/V. Claimed very seriously damaged and probably sunk. Another M/V 6000 tons one direct hit. Badly damaged one DR. Did not fire throughout, possible damaged, one Blenheim damaged by AA. No casualties, 2,500 lb bomb dropped on Spanish Quay, Tripoli, burst observed. All aircraft returned from above operations. [Source: PRO WO 106/240]

Given this rate of attrition it was no wonder that Berlin was told by Admiral Weichold, the German liaison officer with the Italian Navy, that unless there were 'radical changes and immediate measures to remedy the situation [. . .] the entire Italo-German position in North Africa will be lost'. At this stage Hitler refused to withdraw any squadrons from the Eastern Front. However, Fliegerkorps X, which was based in Crete and North Africa, was ordered to give the Axis convoys air cover, but it was not moved back to Sicily. It was spread even more thinly over the Mediterranean and thus unable to launch any attacks on Malta, or indeed afford the convoys effective cover. In a signal to Berlin on 14 September Fliegerkorps X made it very clear that: 'Malta is of the very greatest importance for Britain's attacks on Axis supplies to Africa.'

September 1941: Fortunes of the Malta Convoys

Malta is delighted when another convoy reaches port on the 29th, but thereafter it is increasingly hazardous to get merchant traffic through the Mediterranean.

Fliegerkorps X also informed Berlin that: 'the extraordinary increase in air and submarine activity from Malta' made the dispatch of another supply convoy by the British inevitable. But it was not optimistic about its chances of intercepting such a convoy, as 'in the light of past experiences, even if we keep a continuous watch on shipping in Malta harbours and keep up reccos. over the whole of the Mediterranean between Malta and Alexander the area is so extensive that sightings will be fortuitous.' Nevertheless it was decided that 'exhaustive reconnaissance' should take place and 'all bombers, dive bombers, fighter and heavy fighter units, as far as not engaged on providing protective escort for convoys and important air transports, will be held in readiness.'

The convoy, *Halberd*, sailed from Gibraltar with an impressive escort, which included the *Ark Royal* and the battleship *Nelson*. One young naval officer on the *Nelson* described how: 'all the destroyers are spread out like a vast screen 5,000 yards ahead, the "umbrella" so formed shielding the convoy and a large area in which the *Ark Royal* can operate. *Ark* is keeping eight fighters in the air all day.' On 27 September, however, the *Nelson* was hit by a torpedo on the starboard side. Lieutenant Blundell heard: 'a horrid underwater thud, the whole bow rose and quivered and the ship shook like a mighty animal'. Compartments 43–80 were flooded to the waterline and its speed reduced to 14 knots. Blundell observed that: 'the bow had gone down about six foot, and, looking along the Upper Deck, the ship looks most peculiar, as if she was plunging downhill. If one stands at the stern it looks as if one could step straight off into the sea.' The merchant ship *Imperial Star* was also hit – and so badly that after being towed for two hours she had to be scuttled and then sunk by friendly fire.

Admiral Somerville's Force H was ready to engage with Italian naval forces if they took up their usual position south of Cagliari, 'provided that the primary object which is safe arrival of convoy at its destination' was not jeopardized. This time the Italian Navy did not provoke a sea battle and the merchantmen reached Malta safely. The Admiralty somewhat guardedly congratulated Somerville, but shared 'the disappointment of the Fleet that the enemy's lack of enterprise prevented it being brought to battle'. Possibly Cunningham was commenting on this when he signalled: 'Please accept slap on back from me to compensate for slap on belly with wet fish.'!

In its propaganda radio programmes beamed to Spain and Turkey, the Italian Government observed with considerable truth that: 'the situation in the Mediterranean [for the British] must be serious to expose the Fleet in this manner.'

It was indeed becoming an increasingly risky business dispatching convoys to Malta. In the early autumn Hitler ordered ten U-Boats from the Atlantic to the Mediterranean, which compelled the Admiralty temporarily to suspend the dispatch of any further convoys. Instead it was decided, in October, to send two pairs of unescorted merchantmen through Spanish and French territorial waters with a four-day gap between them. They were to be painted black and 'appear to be in a somewhat lousy condition'. Like chameleons, they would adopt several disguises: initially they would fly Spanish colours, then change to French, and once they reached Cape Bon, hoist the Italian flag. On 30 October the *Empire Pelican* and the *Empire Defender* set sail with Convoy OG-70 for Gibraltar, but parted company shortly before they reached the Straits. Both however were discovered and sunk. The sailing of the next pair of merchant ships, the *Barracuda* and the *Empire Panther* was cancelled, as were plans to send the oil tanker, SS *Thorshavet* through to Malta.

November 1941: A Question of Morale

*In Fortress Malta it is crucial to maintain the morale of
the population. If that collapses, the island could fall.
The lull in the bombing offensive against Malta enables
the Government to prepare for the trials ahead.*

On 12 November the *Ark Royal* was hit and sunk by a German
submarine 30 miles east of Gibraltar. This was a serious loss since
two British carriers were already laid up for repairs as a result of
bomb damage, while a third had been docked after having run
aground. An officer in the wardroom of the *Nelson* tried to make light
of the news when he remarked that: 'when the Italians handed the
chit to Lord Haw Haw, he'd refused to broadcast it, saying that he'd
heard that too many times before . . .' But the stark fact remained
that without a carrier, Force H could no longer run convoys to Malta.
The only cargo ship to get through to Malta was the *Breconshire*,
which arrived in mid-December from Alexandria, carrying oil.
Shortly before Christmas, the Governor ominously informed the
Admiralty that in view of the impossibility of running a convoy to
Malta, 'we must be obviously ready for drastic reductions in issues of
essential commodities.'

Thus no opportunity was lost to bolster the morale of the population. Messages of encouragement and praise were sent by the King,
Churchill and the Colonial Secretary at regular intervals. They were
aimed, as a civil servant at the Colonial Office minuted, at 'keeping
the Maltese people in good fettle'. He went to say that: 'the Maltese
are of a temperament which is undoubtedly encouraged by official
notice.' When Lord Louis Mountbatten visited Malta in April 1941, he
conceived of the dramatic idea of awarding the George Cross to
Malta or the Maltese people 'as a whole'. In London King George VI
liked the idea but felt that it was at the moment premature.

The maintenance of Morale was an important dimension of
Domestic policy. Anyone suspected of pro Italian leanings had
already been arrested in June 1940. By July 1941 some sixty-two
men and twelve women were still interned. Many of them were
prominent citizens: they included a former Chief Justice and a priest,
who was a member of the Cathedral Chapter, as well as the leader
of the Nationalist Party. The Governor was understandably worried

about their release and potential role as Quislings, if Malta were invaded. He pointed out to the Colonial Secretary in July that even if the enemy gained only 'a temporary foothold on the island, the internees might be in a position to direct his special attention to those who had been zealous in combating disloyal activities'. He successfully managed to persuade the Colonial Secretary to send a maximum of forty internees to Uganda for the duration of the war.

The ongoing saga of the ecclesiastical succession to the See of Malta also continued to exercise the Maltese Government. Dobbie candidly observed in February 1941 that: 'recent attacks on Malta have made it necessary to use every available means to keep up the people's morale and influence of the clergy can be invaluable in that respect.' He continued to press for an eventual successor to be appointed to the Archbishopric of Malta. Maltese politics prevented the common sense solution of nominating Gonzi, the Bishop of Gozo, since he was an anathema to the Stricklands and the Constitutional Party, who regarded him as a political enemy and a traitor. Dobbie himself was under pressure from Strickland's paper, the *Times of Malta*, which had been highly critical of the Government's cleaning up operations after the '*Illustrious* blitz'. Although Dobbie was convinced that Gonzi was 'entirely loyal', he realized his appointment would cause 'the acutest dissension in the body politic here', and had little option but to urge the Foreign Office to recommend to the Papacy the appointment of Father Zarb, who was more acceptable to the Stricklands, and more likely not to oppose the planned post-war educational reforms, as coadjutor or assistant, to the ailing Archbishop.

Another factor adversely affecting morale was the steep rise in the cost of living. By 30 September 1941 the cost of living had risen by 75 per cent over the 1939 level, while wages had risen just 35 per cent. In an attempt to redress the balance subsidies were introduced in November 1941. These managed to stabilize prices of such key goods as bread, sugar, lard, margarine and kerosene at pre-war levels.

Nevertheless, there were, as Dobbie informed the Colonial Office, large numbers of Government employees and dock workers who were not earning a living wage. Not surprisingly they were increasingly demanding bonuses to supplement their meagre wages.

December 1941: The Kesselring Offensive

However, there was no provision for discussing matters of common interest between the four official authorities that employed labour: the Government, the Navy, the RAF and the Army, and there was also no Government labour conciliation officer. On 23 November the Dockyard and Imperial Workers' Union complained that Dobbie had refused to see their representatives and merely advised them to talk separately to the relevant Government departments. The leaders deplored this decision and considered that: 'as affecting an issue of extreme importance and urgency the refusal constitutes a negation of those principles of democracy to preserve which we are all fighting and shall continue to fight until victory is achieved'. Behind the scenes, however, Dobbie was strongly urging the British Government to agree to increased subsidies, and on 23 January 1942 the row was defused when it was agreed that workers, whose wage did not exceed 23 shillings a week were to receive a bonus of 8 shillings.

By autumn, with much of the shelter construction programme completed, the Malta Government was able to draw up ambitious plans for building underground workshops in the dockyards, underground supply depots, flour mills and hangers. A fire fighting expert from the UK had also visited the island, but by the time he had drawn up his report in February, Malta was facing a second and much more deadly attack from the Luftwaffe.

December 1941: The Kesselring Offensive

In an attempt to secure the lines of communication between Italy and North Africa, Hitler orders Luftflotte II to Sicily. Kesselring now has the means to neutralize Malta. The raid in the night of 4/5 December 1941 marks the beginning of continuous attacks on Malta for the next five months.

At the end of October 1941 Hitler had taken steps to neutralize Malta by transferring German submarines, mine sweepers and torpedo boats to the Mediterranean. Then a month later the whole of Fliegerkorps II followed, and was put under the command of Field Marshal Kesselring, who was also made Commander-in-Chief South and was specifically entrusted with the 'suppression of Malta'. In the

Campaign Chronicle

week before Christmas the Luftwaffe already began a series of small scale attacks on Malta. On Christmas Eve, for instance, two Ju 88s escorted by twenty fighters, which included Me 109s, attacked the Grand Harbour; while on 19 December the Italians staged a successful torpedo attack on two British battleships, the *Queen Elizabeth* and the *Valiant* in Alexandria harbour. The significance of this was that Admiral Cunningham could no longer hold the Italian battle fleet in check. With the prospect of escalating German air attacks in the New Year Malta was indeed threatened as never before.

Christmas Day 1941 was cold and wet, and was marked by an absence of hostilities on both sides. The only enemy plane to fly over Malta was Italian. It was observed by Pilot Officer Tommy Thompson at Ta' Qali:

> Suddenly an Italian bi-plane appeared zooming over at hedge height, and dropped out a bag with streamers attached right in the middle of the airfield. An armament officer was sent to look at it, but after a brief inspection decided it wasn't a booby trap. Inside was a hand drawn Christmas card of an Italian sitting astride his plane with the inscription 'Happy Christmas to the Gentlemen of the Royal Air Force at Ta' Qali from the Gentlemen of the Regia Aeronautica, Sicily.' [Source: Holland, *Fortress Malta*, p. 207]

As in 1940 Christmas was celebrated as best it could. Despite the ominous outlook, food shortages had not yet begun to bite. Rations had been saved for Christmas meals and children's parties, and rum, which had unaccountably disappeared from the naval stores, found its way onto many civilian tables in all sorts of strange bottles and receptacles. Service personnel were served, as usual, the traditional Christmas meal by their officers. Gunner H. Fleming, for example, enjoyed a slap up meal of egg and bacon for breakfast, followed by pork, greens, plum pudding and beer for dinner.

On Boxing Day hostilities were resumed. Luqa airfield was bombed and German reconnaissance aircraft, escorted by some forty-five fighters, flew over the island at great height. Initially the Luftwaffe's aim, as unveiled by Kesselring at a conference at Luftflotte II's headquarters in February, was to neutralize Malta's

December 1941: The Kesselring Offensive

aerial defence, so that its fighters would be unable to attack the German bombers. The three airfields were to be subjected to heavy bombing and the ground forces eliminated by anti-personnel bombs and machine gun fire. Shipping and the Grand Harbour were also to be subjected to continuous bombing, but as far as possible civilian targets in Valletta were to be spared. During the night tip and run raids by single aircraft were to disrupt clearing up operations and intensify exhaustion by interrupting sleep. Once Malta's defences were destroyed, an invasion could then be considered.

In January there were 262 raids, and in February 236. With the effective employment by the Germans of Me 109s, the RAF was effectively outclassed. On 15 January the AOC, Air Marshal Sir Hugh Lloyd, in a telegram to HQ Middle East, made it very clear that: 'the first problem here is fighter defence', and that he did not hold 'the tools for the job'. The Hurricane II was easily outclassed by the Me 109 in speed and height. Only Spitfires were capable of gaining height sufficiently quickly to match the Me 109. The other problem was that the Ju 88s were so well protected by armoured plating that only Kittyhawks, which were armed with cannon, had any chance of destroying them. Thus, not surprisingly, Lloyd stressed that the 'ultimate answer to defence of this island is 3 squadrons Spitfires, 2 squadrons Kittyhawks and ½ squadron Hurricane IIs for night defence'.

In early February the Air Ministry agreed to the dispatch of a mere 'fourteen or fifteen Spitfires'. Lloyd was informed that only this small quantity could initially be sent because the design of the planes limited the number that could be accommodated on an aircraft carrier. He was therefore given strict orders to 'conserve these aircraft as much as possible [. . .] and restrict their use to essential high flying operations over Malta.' It took a month for them to arrive, and in the meantime the situation steadily deteriorated. When the weather cleared in early February the Me 109s came out 'like summer flies'. They were able to fly round the island almost at will and vastly outnumbered the Hurricanes, which, as one report of this date put it, were 'invariably jumped when covering incoming and outgoing aircraft'.

Protecting incoming shipping was also becoming increasingly difficult as Me 109s were able to engage the Hurricanes in superior

Campaign Chronicle

The Inadequacy of the RAF

The inadequacy of the RAF was clearly shown on 22 February 1942. Lloyd sent the following description the next day to HQ RAF Middle East:

> Continuous alerts. Attacks on aerodromes all day. Apart from material damage to buildings, aircraft, aerodromes and runways, which is very serious, loss of working time is very grave. Loading of mines onto 37 squadron aircraft, for example, had not been completed at nightfall. It largely accounts for bad serviceability among fighters and reconnaissance aircraft [. . .] Our fighters did gallant work, but pace and numbers too hot for them. [Source: PRO AIR 23/1200]

numbers, while the Ju 88s could concentrate on bombing the ships and the harbour. Lloyd constantly stressed that Malta desperately needed Spitfires for high cover and Hurricanes armed with cannon so that they could penetrate the armoured plating of the German bombers. Once the RAF possessed these, he was confident that: 'if we could shoot down a score, this daylight nonsense would stop.'

The longed for Spitfires were not to appear until 7 March. In the meantime the erosion of Malta's defences continued and her position as a staging post for aircraft to the Middle East was threatened, as aircraft landing to refuel were vulnerable to constant German attacks, which also took their toll on the pilots, the troops manning the anti-aircraft guns and the personnel working on the airfields. Gunner Fleming, who was working as a telephonist at the RA HQ: 'was now reaching a stage where I used to dread the sound of the siren. When the alert went, my hands grew cold and numb, every nerve in my body became painfully cramped, and if I was on duty I was never able to concentrate during the raid . . .' By 6 February AOC Malta reported that eighty-seven pilots were sick or non-effective and that 'new blood' was urgently required. A reinforcement of fifteen

January 1942: The Air Battle Continues

pilots trained to fly Spitfires was sent by flying boat and arrived at dawn on 16 February, with the promise that more would arrive when possible.

On 23 February the Joint Intelligence Committee informed the War Cabinet that incessant air attacks had resulted in 'partial neutralization of the island'. Malta's position was made the more vulnerable by the retreat of the Eighth Army in North Africa and the loss of the aerodromes in North West Cyrenaica.

January 1942: The Air Battle Continues

Until a sufficient number of Spitfires can be sent to Malta, it is no exaggeration to say that the main defence of the island devolves upon the AA units and the troops working on the airfields.

Initially there had been some friction between the RAF and the Army on the island. The soldiers were jealous of the way the RAF seemed to be getting all the publicity, while young RAF pilots were critical of the soldiers for apparently doing nothing. The heavy raids in January and February 1942 changed these perceptions.

It was essential if any aircraft were to survive that protective pens should be built, which would shield them from anything but a direct hit. Air Vice Marshal Lloyd conceded after the Battle of Malta had been won that: 'I'd have been out of business but for the soldiers.' About 2,500–3,000 soldiers were divided into working parties on the three airfields. The Royal West Kents and the Buffs were based at Luqa, the Manchesters at Ta' Qali and the Devons at Hal Far. Within three months they managed to lay 27 miles of dispersal runways, and construct fourteen large bomber pens, 170 fighter pens, seventy reconnaissance aircraft pens and thirty-one naval aircraft pens. They worked in twelve-hour shifts, only taking cover during raids. Colonel Westropp used a motor cycle to do his rounds when he inspected his working parties and recalled later how: 'I used to leave the strip when I saw them scatter as I could not hear the approach of the bombers, because of the noise of the engine. I then laid the cycle on its side and prepared to hug the ground and made myself as flat and small as possible.'

Initially sandbags were used for the aircraft pens, but these were

59

Campaign Chronicle

later replaced by petrol cans and oil drums filled with stones and earth. Finally, rubble and masonry from the bombed sites was used. The most ingenious dispersal runway was the Safi strip, which linked the airfields of Luqa and Hal Far. In the almost lyrical words of the historian of *The Air Battle of Malta*:

> it is a track winding through grey rock, small terraced fields, carob trees and scrub. Here and there are small farm houses built like fortresses in the days when the Maltese farmer had to defend himself against Arab marauders, and guarded by clumps of prickly pear. Many tons of bombs have been dropped upon the strip, and it was often considered an adventure to travel the length of it unless guided by someone who new all the shelter holes. Throughout its length pens were built in an intricate pattern, making the best use of the lie of the land. [Source: *The Air Battle of Malta*, p. 48]

General Beak, the GOC Land Forces in Malta was only pointing out the obvious when he wrote in March that: 'for some considerable time practically the whole of the air defence of Malta had devolved upon the anti-aircraft artillery and searchlights.' In the first three months of the Kesselring offensive the Germans frequently changed their tactics and forced the AA to respond accordingly. The Ju 88s often varied the height at which they would pull out of their dives, forcing the AA constantly to recalculate the settings for their barrages. The Luftwaffe was often helped by the cover provided by a cloudy sky. To combat this the 'Xmas barrage' was evolved, whereby each of the batteries fired into a different square in the rough form of a Five of Diamonds. It proved a considerable deterrent to the accuracy of German bombers, since it provided both density and depth.

At night, there was considerable difficulty in coordinating the AA's fire with the activity of the RAF, as there were often Wellingtons, Fulmers, Hurricanes and transport planes airborne over Malta. One evening the RAF controller ordered the AA to stop firing as the position of one Wellington over the island was not known, but this merely enabled the Germans to press home their attacks on the harbour, with the subsequent loss of HMS *Mori*. To avoid a recurrence AA fire was divided into three phases:

February 1942: The Demand for Spitfires

- Initially the guns had complete freedom to fire at any target anywhere above the island.
- Then if aircraft were taking off, the guns would fire only over a certain part of the island.
- Finally when British aircraft were returning from a mission fire would be limited only to cover the Grand Harbour.

February 1942: The Demand for Spitfires

Malta desperately needs more Spitfires to contest control of the skies by the superior numbers of the German Luftwaffe.

Plans were drawn up for the dispatch of sixteen Spitfires on 27 February. They were fitted with long-range jettisonable tanks and thus had a minimum sea range of 890 sea miles. But a potential defect in the tanks was discovered and at the last moment they had to be transported back to Gibraltar by the *Eagle*. In all except one Spitfire the faults were remedied and on 7 March the first batch of fifteen Spitfires were at last flown off the *Eagle*, and 'rendezvoused' with a force of eight Blenheims. Potentially this was a hazardous operation, as the Blenheims could only take off from Gibraltar in daylight, and were cumbersome and slow, and to quote the report from Force H on the operation, noted 'for the irregularity of their time keeping'. However, on this occasion, all worked well and the Spitfires were able to reach Ta' Qali in daylight.

Within hours Ta' Qali was heavily bombed, but mercifully the Spitfires were not damaged. Before they could go into action their brown–grey camouflage needed to be replaced by a grey–blue colour, which was more appropriate for Malta, and their guns needed to be aligned so the bullets would converge on a single target. On the 10th they were scrambled for the first time, and were able to use tactics that had been successful in the Battle of Britain: the Hurricanes were sent to deal with the bombers while the Spitfires, rapidly climbing to a height of 19,000 feet, took on the escorts. For the first time the RAF had the advantage over the Me 109s. One of these was shot down and at least another damaged: but a mere fifteen Spitfires were hardly going to win the Battle of Malta single-handed!

Campaign Chronicle

Ten days later the situation was as dangerous as it had ever been. Lloyd painted a bleak picture:

> Our much attenuated fighter force putting up a super effort against great odds. But it is impossible to go on. Unable [to] get near bombers owing [to] heavy escort. Attacks are sustained and time arrives when fighters must land, when they are bombed, making refuelling and rearming very difficult [. . .] Also grave risk [of] damage to aircraft. It amounts to one sortie by all our fighters in sustained attack of several hours with varying number of fighter escort, all greater than ours. Also have to cover all outgoing and incoming reconnaissance day delivery and sea rescues. [Source: PRO AIR 20/2428]

Plans had been drawn up for a further thirty-two Spitfires to be flown to Malta by Operation *Picket*, but the Navy had only the capacity to send a further sixteen. The aircraft were sent crated to the *Eagle*, where ground crews working in claustrophobic conditions – with only inches to spare between each machine – had assembled them. On 21 March the sixteen Spitfires were ready to take off for Malta in two flights. One fighter pilot, Tim Johnston, remembered the breezy instructions they were given after a breakfast of bream:

> A flight was to go off in the first batch – you needn't worry about that chaps, it's a piece of cake [. . .] we ought to begin to be careful near Bizerta, the French sometimes sent fighters out and you never knew what they might do; while passing Pantelleria, it was advisable to keep a bloody good look out. They had RDF there and a squadron of 109s.

However, despite arriving at Malta in the middle of a raid, they were able to land intact at Luqa.

Although these were welcome reinforcements, Lloyd and Dobbie, who emphasized that the situation remained extremely serious, both pressed for another thirty-two Spitfires, and from then on a regular

March 1942: Running the Axis Blockade

monthly reinforcement of sixteen. In the immediate future the most that could be scratched up was a further sixteen Spitfires that were flown in the second part of Operation *Picket* on 29 March, and ten-cannon Hurricanes armed with cannons. The problem was not that the Air Ministry was reluctant to send them but that, as the RAF in Egypt had none to spare, all reinforcements had to come in from the West. HMS *Eagle* was also scheduled to be laid up temporarily for repairs and the only remaining aircraft carrier in Force H, the *Argus*, was too small to carry Spitfires.

March 1942: Running the Axis Blockade

With the Royal Navy stretched to breaking point in the Mediterranean, the British seek American aid in transporting Spitfires to Malta. Meanwhile, the German noose tightens around the island, making the running of convoys increasingly hazardous.

Given the absence of a suitable British carrier, Air Marshal Sir Charles Portal raised at the Chiefs of Staff meetings of 23 and 24 March 1942 the possibility of an American aircraft carrier being used on a temporary basis. The First Lord of the Admiralty agreed and the C-in-C of the Home Fleet was ordered to make contact with the US C-in-C, European Waters. On 1 April Churchill contacted Roosevelt directly and informed him that: 'it seems likely from extra-ordinary enemy concentration on Malta that they hope to exterminate our air defence in time to reinforce either Libya or their Russian offensive.' He went on to stress that since the *Eagle* was laid up for a month as a results of faults in her steering gear, and that the other carrier, the *Argus*, was both too small and too slow (and also had to provide the cover for the carrier launching the Spitfires), the use of the American *Wasp*, which could carry some fifty Spitfires in one go, was the only way Malta could be saved. Initially Roosevelt queried whether the British carrier *Furious*, which was scheduled to leave the USA after a refit on 3 April, could carry out the operation, but readily agreed to the use of the *Wasp* when told the *Furious* was manned by only a skeleton crew.

Forty-seven Spitfires were embarked at Grenock in record time on

63

Campaign Chronicle

13 April. The plan was to steam through the Straits of Gibraltar at night so as to avoid the notice of enemy agents in Spain and North Africa, and then fly off some 700 miles from Malta. The pilots, except for Squadron Leader Gracie, were all young men who were new to Malta. One of them, Dennis Barnham, remembers Gracie ominously telling him: 'if you are lucky enough to fly you're generally outnumbered forty or fifty to one.' On Monday 20 April the planes flew off the aircraft carrier and reached Malta, as was now the norm, in the midst of an air raid. In his diary Barnham recalled:

> approaching some steep hills clustered thick with buildings that protrude in the sea; its a harbour and there is a ship down there, low in the water, smoke coming from it. Peering down on top of its fore-shortened black masts I look deep into its splintered hold; tiny flames are dancing in it; its blackened with fire.

Only ninety minutes after the Spitfires had landed the Germans intensified their attacks on Ta' Qali and Luqa, and both airfields were reduced to a 'complete shambles'. On 23 April Dobbie informed Churchill that seventeen Spitfires had been destroyed on the ground and twenty-nine more damaged, either while they were on the ground or else in combat. Ominously he added that: 'we can at the moment only put six Spitfires into the air.'

In contrast to the professionalism and deadly effectiveness of the Luftwaffe, the incoming British pilots had no experience of fighting over Malta, and well over half had never flown in combat before. Once they arrived in Malta they were thrown into battle without any acclimatization or pre-combat training. Barnham, who had fought in the Battle of Britain, asked his Squadron Leader what were the best tactics to use. In reply he was given the following terse advice:

> You'll learn, but don't go chasing the b—s all the way to Sicily [. . .] If you're by yourself weave around at nought feet all over the island or better still do steep turns in the middle of Ta' Qali aerodrome inside the ring of Bofors guns [. . .] but don't take any notice of the fighters, its the big boys we've got to kill.

March 1942: Running the Axis Blockade

Clearly there was no alternative to the dispatch of another batch of Spitfires. Churchill again contacted Roosevelt for a repeat use of the *Wasp* to deliver 'a good sting'. When it was granted, he minuted that he should be informed of 'the programme for feeding Malta with Spits, week by week, during the next eight weeks'. On 9 May a combined *Wasp–Eagle* operation took place, when forty-seven Spitfires from the *Wasp* and seventeen from the *Eagle* were flown off west of Gibraltar to Malta. All except four arrived (see page 77).

Although renewed Luftwaffe attacks had commenced on Malta in December 1941, it was still easier to pass convoys to the island in January than it had been in the previous three months because Axis airfields had been captured in the bulge of Cyrenaica. Since Malta had grown in importance as a base for attacking Axis convoys to North Africa, the demands for depth charges, bombs, torpedoes, benzene and aviation spirit had grown. It was also vital to build up the supplies of wheat, kerosene and a whole range of other foods and materials for the civilian population. Hovering over Malta was also the threat of invasion, should the Germans succeed in breaking her air defences. To meet this, a further thirty Bofors guns with crews, two more battalions of British troops and fourteen cruiser tanks were earmarked for dispatch to Malta.

In early January HMS *Glengyle* and the *Breconshire*, which effectively ran an oil shuttle service from Alexandria, had successfully delivered cargoes of heavy and light oils. On 16 January Convoy MF-3 sailed from Alexandria after an unexpected delay caused by an unpredicted gale and sandstorm, and the destroyer *Kingston* fouling the boom and then being rammed by the *Foxhound*. The convoy was composed of four merchant ships, accompanied by the anti-aircraft cruiser, the *Carlisle*, and eight destroyers. German intelligence was well aware of the convoy, and on the 17th one of the escorts, the *Ghurkha*, was sunk by a German submarine. But as a result of effective air cover given by No. 201, Naval Cooperation Group, based at the Benghazi airfields, three merchant ships and their escorts reached the Grand Harbour on the 19th. The fourth merchant ship, the *Thermopylae*, developed engine trouble and had to be detached from the main convoy and sent to Benghazi. On the way she was bombed and had to be sunk. Most of her crew were saved, but a third of the Bofors guns were lost and nearly half the number of tanks. The three ships, however, were successfully unloaded, as cloud cover prevented heavy enemy attacks.

On 27 January the *Breconshire* safely reached Malta, and the *Glengyle* and *Rowellan Castle* were escorted back to Alexandria in Convoy MF-4. All in all MF-3 and 4 were successful operations, but it was to be much more difficult for the next major convoy. By the end of January Axis forces had again seized the western Cyrenaican airfields and Malta's fighter forces were being remorselessly eroded by the Luftwaffe. Yet, as Malta's needs were as urgent as ever, and over 2,000 troops and much equipment were still waiting to be shipped to the island, Cunningham was prepared to risk another convoy.

MF-5, which consisted of three merchantmen, the *Carlisle* and eight destroyers, sailed from Alexandria on 12 February. The intention was to give Axis forces the impression that it was heading for Tobruk. The convoy sailed in two sections, which would meet up off Tobruk at nightfall, and then follow a north-westerly route across the central basin to Malta, well out of the range of German dive bombers. Crucially no fighter cover could be given by the RAF, and the Navy alone was responsible for its defence. The plan worked well until the evening of 13 February when the *Clan Campbell* was bombed and had to be sent into Tobruk. The following day the *Clan Chatton* was sunk and the engines of the *Rowellan Castle* were disabled so badly she had to be sunk, as there was no prospect of getting her into harbour. The Vice Admiral, Malta, wrote in his official War Diary: 'Subsequent reconnaissance showed that a strong enemy cruiser force was endeavouring to intercept and had *Rowellan Castle* not been sunk a worse disaster would almost certainly have occurred.'

Cunningham drew the conclusion from the failure of MF-5 that it 'appears useless to pass in a convoy until the air situation in Malta and the military situation in Cyrenaica has been restored'. But this logical, albeit rather defeatist view, was not shared by the Chiefs of Staff. On 18 February they received a grim communication from Dobbie, which stressed that the 'non arrival of MF-5' had 'accentuated a supply situation which is already unsatisfactory'. The general position was that supplies would last only until June, but petrol and

March 1942: Running the Axis Blockade

submarine diesel oil were down to just two months. Meanwhile, 'All service and civil expenditure had been cut to the bone' and vital army training was 'almost at a standstill' in an attempt to conserve resources. The minimum required to prevent stocks falling below the existing level was 15,000 tons a month. In view of the Axis control of the bases in Cyrenaica Dobbie considered it essential 'to explore seriously and urgently [. . .] all other means of getting supplies not only from east but west also'.

The Chiefs of Staff were alarmed by the situation in Malta and four days later came to the conclusion that: 'clearly we must, in spite of the difficulties, transport to Malta what is really indispensable for the continuance of operations and the maintenance of civilian morale. If we do not so, we must face the fact that operations will probably cease after the end of June.' The War Cabinet's Joint Planning Staff then drew up a series of recommendations for supplying Malta. Convoys were to be supplemented by various 'unorthodox methods' such as:

- The use of C class cruisers with their ammunition and armaments reduced to a minimum.
- The use of the old wireless-controlled target ship, the *Centurion*, which could be disguised as a foreign merchantman.
- Supplies could also be moved by small coastal craft from Palestine, Syria and Egypt.
- The increased use of submarines and minelayers for carrying vital spares.
- The use of the Special Operations Executive to secure supplies of fodder from French North Africa.
- Contacts with Turkish suppliers arranged through the UK Commercial Corporation there.
- And finally the increased use of aircraft for 'small bulk' items.

The upshot of this was that on 28 February 1942 the Chiefs of Staff instructed the Commanders-in Chief, Middle East to make: 'a further attempt to pass a convoy in [the] March dark period. No consideration of risk to ships themselves need deter you from this. During the progress of this operation it should be regarded as your primary military commitment.'

Campaign Chronicle

Convoy MW-10 sailed from Alexandria on 20 March. It consisted of three fast merchant ships, the *Pampas*, *Clan Campbell* and the *Talabot*, a Norwegian vessel, and the *Breconshire*, and was again escorted by the anti-aircraft cruiser, *Carlisle* and six more destroyers. It was preceded by six small destroyers of the Hunter class, which were to conduct an anti-submarine sweep. Meanwhile, a further force of destroyers and cruisers under Rear Admiral Vian set sail in the evening and met up with the convoy the following day. The convoy passed though the danger area between Crete and Cyrenaica without incident – largely because of a series of diversionary raids by the Eighth Army and attacks by the RAF and Fleet Air Arm on Axis airfields in Cyrenaica – but it was spotted by a German transport aircraft. On 22 March the Italian Fleet put out to sea from Taranto to intercept MW-10.

Initially the convoy was attacked by both Italian and German planes. Then, shortly before 2pm, two destroyers and heavy cruisers of the Italian Fleet were sighted. Behind them, but out of sight, were two more destroyers, a light cruiser and the battleship, *Littorio*. According to a prearranged and much practised plan, the convoy under escort turned away to the south-west, while Rear Admiral Vian's force turned north to lay a smoke screen, which effectively protected the convoy. There was a brief exchange of fire but the smoke screen saved Vian's ships from the superior Italian fire power. At 6pm Admiral Iachino managed to circle round the smoke screen and head south to where the convoy was steaming towards Malta. The *Littorio* badly damaged two destroyers, but a combination of bad weather, the other destroyers closing to 600 yards, where they could bring their 4½-inch guns to bear, and then a torpedo attack from the *Cleopatra*, caused Iachino to break off contact and return to port.

The naval authorities in Malta had no clear picture as to when, or in what order, the ships would reach the Grand Harbour. Despite thick cloud, German air attacks on the convoy began about 7am. British fighters based at Malta could offer little protection. Such was the damage that had been done to the airfields by German bombing that only five fighters were actually operational! It was not until 9.20am that German aircraft managed to hit the *Breconshire*, which was only 5 miles from the entrance to the Grand Harbour, with three bombs. Her engine room was flooded and her steering disabled. HMS

March 1942: Running the Axis Blockade

Penelope managed to get her in tow with a 6½-inch hawser, but this soon broke apart and the *Breconshire* drifted into shore. Fortunately she passed through the south-eastern corner of the minefield safely and the following day managed to anchor off Marsaxlokk. Destroyers were detailed to guard her and the Army set up an extra battery of AA guns to cover her. She had a large number of passengers onboard, who because of the bad weather could not be immediately disembarked. *Talabot* and *Pampas* sailed into the Grand Harbour safely about 9.30am, but the *Clan Campbell* was hit in the engine room and sank. Her captain went down with the ship, but her escort, HMS *Eridge* managed to save 112 of her crew.

The decision was taken by Vice Admiral Leatham not to employ servicemen to unload on the grounds that the Maltese stevedores were much more used to the work and could consequently unload a ship twice as fast. Work started immediately on unloading the *Talabot* and *Pampas* by hand, and thanks to the low cloud and the AA batteries, neither ship was damaged by further bombing. Although the *Breconshire* was subjected to repeated attacks on the 25th, two tugs, the *Ancient* and the *Robust*, were sent out to tow her into harbour under cover of darkness: but it was not until 11.40 the following day that she was finally secured safely to No.1 Buoy in Marsaxlokk. Again it was misty weather that saved her from attack. Her crew, according to the official narrative of operations, were in a state of 'nearly complete exhaustion – without light, water or cooking facilities'. They were given permission to abandon the ship temporarily, and were fed and given accommodation at the barracks at Kalafrana.

On the following day a series of devastating raids took place on the Grand Harbour. The *Talabot* and the *Pampas* received direct hits amidships and were set on fire: the latter burning until 7pm. The fire floats and the tug *Ancient*, were also well on the way to extinguishing the fire in the *Talabot* when a fresh raid put both fire floats out of action and damaged the tug so badly she had to be towed away and beached. The fire in the *Talabot* then became uncontrollable, and there was the very real danger that the ammunition she was carrying would explode. Admiral Leatham had little option but to have her scuttled. In addition the *Penelope* and the *Avondale* were also damaged, and severe damage was done to the dockyard. Once

Why Were the Ships not Unloaded More Quickly?

The Germans had succeeded in destroying MW-10 in harbour. From the *Pampas* and the *Talabot* only 1,800 tons had been unloaded from a maximum of 16,418. Was the Luftwaffe's victory a foregone conclusion? Increasingly Dobbie was criticized for not using troops and service personnel and working around the clock. It was true that Maltese stevedores did work much more quickly, but as civilians they were not trained to work during air raids. Particularly at night they ran for cover at the first warning siren. Consequently Leatham, after consulting with the Divisional Sea Transport Officer and 'taking all things into consideration', took the fatal decision 'that unloading should be done by day only'. In this he was supported by both Dobbie and Lloyd, but retrospectively it was a major error, as it failed to exploit the opportunities provided by three relatively quiet nights. Only Wing Commander Powell-Sheldon, the Station Commander at Luqa, seized the opportunity on the night of 23/24 to send down some ground crews to unload vital spares for the Wellingtons. Two nights later he rang both Lloyd and Dobbie and drew their attention to the opportunities that were being missed, but his fears were dismissed. It was only after the severe air raids of 26 March that Leatham decided that unloading must go on round the clock, day and night, and 100 men from the Cheshires and a party of naval ratings were ordered 'to augment and give heart to the stevedores in [the] *Pampas*', which was the only ship where work could at present proceed. This was a classic case of shutting the stable door after the horse had bolted, but as some slight consolation 3,970 tons were eventually recovered from the *Pampas* and 1,032 tons from the *Talabot*. It was found that many of the sacks of flour could be retrieved as the water had only penetrated by an inch or so.

again the *Breconshire* was hit and began to burn. Initially it seemed that the fire was extinguished, but the following morning the flames flared up again. In the end an attempt was made to save the oil and get the ship to settle on an even keel by flooding the boiler room in No. 1 Hold and by opening up the stern with a depth charge. Unfortunately the depth charge was inaccurately set and did not explode. In his report Admiral Leatham concluded:

> At about 1100 [hours] this fine and gallant ship heeled over to port and settled on her side, leaving about 10 feet of the starboard side above water, through which it is hoped the oil and some of the stores will be recoverable.
>
> I consider much credit is due to Captain Huchison, his officers and men for the fight they put up to keep the enemy off and their ship afloat. They worked with this hope in front of them until they were practically exhausted, with the most limited resources and under living conditions which would have disheartened a less stout-hearted company. [Source: PRO ADM 116 4559]

Of the convoy escorts that arrived at Malta, HMS *Legion* and *Southwold* were sunk and the *Kingston* and *Penelope* severely damaged. HMS *Carlisle*, *Beaufort*, *Hurworth* and *Eridge* sailed for Alexandria on 25th, while *Avondale* and *Aurora* departed four days later.

Concluding his dispatch on 'The Arrival of the M.W. 10 and Malta at Bay' Leatham observed:

> In spite of all that was done so well, there must remain in my mind the grief that such a large portion of what had been fought so successfully through to the shores of Malta was lost after its safe arrival in harbour. We were just not strong enough.

The immediate consequence of this debacle for Malta was that the Admiralty drew the conclusion, on 4 April, that it would not be possible to run another convoy from either east or west until the RAF had been strongly reinforced on Malta. Three weeks later Dobbie

Campaign Chronicle

was instructed by the C-in-C Middle East to 'place garrison and population on lowest possible scale of rations forthwith . . .'

April 1942: The German Onslaught

Having drawn up plans for an invasion of Malta, the Germans unleash a massive air assault on the island, which bears comparison with the Battle of Britain in intensity and number of enemy planes involved. The island is daily attacked by 200–300 planes, and by mid-April the RAF has only six combat fighters fully operational at any one time. For a short time the Germans achieve their aim and neutralize Malta from the air.

In mid-October 1941 the possibility of landing a force of 35–40,000 troops on Malta was discussed at a joint Italian–German naval conference, and General Roatta, the Chief of Staff of the Italian Army was ordered to draft a paper on the occupation of Malta under the code name of 'C3'. Little progress was made until early January as a result of the British *Crusader* offensive in North Africa. However on 6/7 January 1942 General Cavallero, Chief of the Italian *Commando Supremo* ordered that a 'programme be drawn up forthwith' and training schedules were worked out. The Italians aimed at an invasion in July–August 1942, but Kesselring, who was planning to launch an 'intensified air assault' on Malta at the end of March, was convinced that a landing should follow immediately before the island could recover from the blitz. The Germans managed to gain Mussolini's consent to a surprise attack from the air by parachutists any time 'after the end of May'.

On 31 March the British Intelligence Committee noted: 'there had been a reliable report that approval for the assault had been given by Hitler'. In fact Hitler and Jodl (Head of the German High Command) were highly sceptical of the Italian plans, as they believed that in reality Italy had no intention of launching an invasion. However, if by any chance they did – and provided there were no enemy landings in France or Norway – the Germans were willing to contribute one or two paratroop regiments and some torpedo boats and mine sweepers. One complication was that the Germans were

April 1942: The German Onslaught

also anxious to get on and plan the Tobruk offensive for the end of May or early June at the latest. Kesselring informed the C-in-C Luftwaffe that 'the Malta–Tobruk attack or vice versa must be launched successively because our air forces will not suffice for concurrent offensives.'

Mussolini wanted Malta invaded at the end of May, and on 18 April Hitler actually approved the plan, which was code-named *Hercules*. General Student, the officer commanding the German Fliegerkorps XI, arrived in Rome to begin detailed planning. On 30 April at the German–Italian summit Hitler promised Mussolini 'generous German participation', but on the advice of Rommel, who warned of the growing strength of the British Eighth Army, he suggested Tobruk should be seized first, and only then, Malta invaded. Mussolini agreed, giving the Italian and German planners another two months. But the great disadvantage of the plan was that the link between it and the air offensive was broken, as much of the Luftwaffe was scheduled to be withdrawn to Russia or Africa in May.

The German planning staffs in Italy produced a series of scenarios, which according to one German historian, 'presented a picture of bewildering diversity and afforded little hope that all the Italian and German authorities would quickly agree on a single plan'. When General Student reported to Hitler at the Führer's Headquarters on 21 May, Hitler – according to eyewitness *Fregattenkapitän* Junge – responded 'dramatically and very derogatorily', heaping insults on his Italian allies. He distrusted their security and had 'absolutely no faith' in their navy, as it turned tail whenever the British Alexandria Squadron appeared. He was also sceptical as to whether the sea routes would be any more secure after the capture of Malta, and went on to say that he would not allow any German engineers to sail on Italian ships. General Student rashly declared that he could seize Malta with his paratroopers alone, but Hitler was unimpressed, replying that there was no question of an invasion in 1942. Student was ordered not to return to Rome.

Nevertheless planning continued in the Italian capital, and the provision of assault craft and barges was organized. But once Tobruk fell on 21 June, both Mussolini and Hitler gave the go-ahead for a 'push to Suez'. And when Rommel's Afrikakorps reached El Alamein on 30 June, its requirements were given priority over the projected Malta invasion, which three weeks later were discontinued 'for the time being'.

Without any doubt April was, to quote the words of the official historian, 'the time of the island's greatest trial'. Some 9,500 sorties were flown against the island, over 6,700 tons of bombs were dropped and 11,450 buildings were damaged or destroyed. Fortunately, as a result of the Government's shelter programme, there were sufficient shelters for the population, and consequently a relatively low number of 300 civilians were killed and 330 seriously injured. By early May Malta was neutralized, her harbour destroyed and her aerodromes put out of action for hours at a time. On 26 April the Tenth Submarine Flotilla moved to Alexandria and the air striking force had been rendered virtually impotent.

The cables from Dobbie, Leatham and Lloyd all tell the tale of unrelenting destruction. On 7 April, for instance, the naval authorities reported that the Grand Harbour had been reduced to a shambles:

HMS Penelope *or 'Pepperpot' Escapes Destruction*

Some repair work did manage to continue despite the bombs. Welders from the Royal Engineers managed to patch up the *Penelope* in one of the dry docks, even though bombing had so seriously damaged the dry dock that only constant pumping could keep the water out. When the pumps failed, *Penelope*'s crew and the sappers continued to work until the water was up to their shoulders. In the nick of time the dockyard staff managed to repair the pumps and she was made ready to limp out to Gibraltar. Not before, however, her captain and Gunnery officer had been wounded and all her AA ammunition used up. Eventually at 9.30pm she was able to sail out of harbour, 'battered, dishevelled and with a thousand wooden pegs plugging her splintered wooden sides', but, to quote Leatham, a magnificent example of what can be achieved by 'faith and determination'.

April 1942: The German Onslaught

Hamilton inner wharf blocked by [a Greek submarine] *Glaucos*, No. 2 and 3 boiler yard machinery shop demolished. Santa Teresa tunnel completely wrecked. Sewage system and water supplies almost completely out of action. Temporary engineering and electrical departments, drawing offices and many other offices and store houses have been destroyed. The residences on top of Sheer Bastion and buildings on St Michael's Bastion are completely wrecked [. . .] Numerous large craters in roadways and on wharves and large masses of masonry in roadways which have brought practically all wheeled traffic to a standstill. These are filled or cleared as soon as possible but seldom possible to obtain clearance before further similar raids [. . .] At present there is practically no power or light anywhere in the dockyard except in 4 and 5 dock area. Very few of the essential telephones are in operation. Visual communication employing naval signalmen has been established across French Creek. [Source: PRO WO 106/ 2113]

The intensity of the raids increased still further in the second week in April. At first the Grand Harbour remained the major target, but as April wore on the catalogue of destruction lengthened. Military barracks and camps at St Andrew's, St George's and Ghain Tuffeqha were severely damaged, as were the RAOC's clothing store and the RASC's radio workshop and the fire instrument workshop. The building that housed the records of the Governor's headquarters was hit, as were several brigade headquarters and messes. AA gun positions were also dive bombed and machine gunned. One of the theatre nurses of the Military Hospital at Imtarfa remembered later how a gun position 'just below our officers' mess received a direct hit and terribly wounded survivors were put into an open lorry and driven straight to us'.

The airfields also continued to be subjected to constant bombardment. This reached a peak on 20 April when the Spitfire reinforcements from the *Wasp* flew in. The Germans sent in 306 bombers in one day to destroy them. The impact of the bombs blew in the protective walls of the blast pens onto the Spitfires and thus managed to put them out of action. By 22 April there were only six

Campaign Chronicle

Spitfires still operational, and as soon as others were repaired, they were damaged either by Stukas or Me 109s or by running into one of the many bomb craters on the airfield.

Not only were attacks directed against legitimate military targets but there was also a systematic attempt to break the morale of the people by bombing the civilian population. There were raids on Easter Day as people were going to church, and a few days later on 7 April there was a massive attack on Valletta. Gunner Fleming managed to take cover in a shelter: 'filled almost to suffocation. For nearly an hour we sat in that shelter with our fingers in our ears and biting our lips.' The *Times of Malta* painted a grim picture: Valetta is a stricken city [. . .] all the beautiful old palaces are bombed, all the churches have been ruined, blitzed [. . .] hundreds of houses are no more [. . .] nearly all shops are destroyed . . .'

The military hospital at Imtarfa was also a target. A nurse later remembered how the 'Messerschmitt fighters used to play hide and seek down the blocks of the barrack hospital and machine gun bullets used to fly.' Despite having a red cross on its roof, the dining hall of General Hospital No. 39 was hit on 25 April and six were killed and two wounded. One German POW in the hospital, *Leutnant* Rosenvelt, was horrified by the attack and according to official reports 'behaved well assisting [the] injured after the attack'.

The raids increasingly settled into a pattern. The bombers were escorted by Me 109s, which also frequently carried out machine gun attacks on any suitable target. Colonel Westropp noted dryly in his memoirs that: 'the Me 109s were for sometime in April very insolent, flying low and all around us. There were usually three, and sometimes four, main raids a day, and these were interspersed with minor raids both day and night.' According to the nurse at Imtarfa:

> the raids occurred with clockwork regularity. The enemy appeared at 7am, midday and 6pm. We used to watch the first as we were scrambling to get dressed for breakfast; we spent the second raid in the theatre or the mess, according to whether we went to first or second lunch; and if there were casualties to do during the afternoon we planned whether we would be finished before the 'six o'clock raid'; we usually

April 1942: The German Onslaught

made that raid an interlude for tea. [Source: *Nursing Times*, 16 September 1944]

Until the arrival of the second lot of Spitfires from the *Wasp* and the *Eagle* on 9 May the RAF was hopelessly outnumbered and no longer able to defend the island. On 22 April, for instance, there were only six Spitfires left in Malta and just one at Ta' Qali. There were simply not enough planes for the pilots, who often spent their days helping to construct aircraft pens. Tim Johnston often wondered what the Maltese thought 'at seeing so many pilots on the ground during raids' and overheard one saying: 'that he could not understand why we had to rely on the barrage when there were 150 Spits to take off; another – an omniscient small boy– that we had only eight left'.

Nevertheless the RAF did continue to engage the Germans, and usually managed to inflict significant casualties. On 25 April, for instance, the planes based at Ta' Qali shot down five German aircraft and damaged about nine others at the cost of one Hurricane and, according to Squadron Leader Lord David Douglas Hamilton, 'a few others with bullet holes or other damage'. The nature of the fighting over Malta was very different from over Europe, where by 1942 the norm was to deploy mass fighter sweeps composed of several squadrons. Over Malta the key was to gain height as soon as possible and then aim for the German bombers. The handful of British planes was directed from the ground by Group Captain Woodhall or 'Woody'. David Douglas Hamilton recorded in his diary on 30 April Woodhall's advice and how he reacted to it:

'Big jobs (bombers) now fifteen miles north of Grand Harbour coming south. Many little jobs (fighters) over the island.' Then later, 'Party has now split into three and are coming over St Paul's Bay, Grand Harbour and Kalafrana.' At the right moment, he said, 'Come in now and come in fast.'

Down we went at about 400mph into the middle of the 88s, just as they finished their dive . . . [Source: James Douglas-Hamilton, *The Air Battle For Malta*, p. 47]

The fighting was a mass of confused dog fights, which took place at great speed and in which the overwhelming strength of the Germans was brought to bear. The Me 109s always worked in pairs, so they could cover each other. Nine days earlier Dennis Barnham was flying above 'five, seven, ten, twenty' Junkers, 'all sizes, extending in depth downward like fishes in a tank'. He dived and hit one in the port engine, and then was overwhelmed by Messerschmitts. Later he described the encounter in his diary:

> 109s! Two, head-on views, diving from my left, blinking with light. Curling blue tracers strand about me as I turn towards them. A third – got my sight on him for an instant before he went under my nose [. . .] Two more from the right this time. Turn in towards them [. . .] can't turn sharply enough [. . .] Another 109 below me. Drop onto his tail. I'll get him all right. A gigantic shape, all rivets and oil streaks, the underside of a Messerschmitt blots out the sky! But I am still on a 109's tail [. . .] My aircraft shudders and shudders and shudders as I pour bullets into it. It bursts with black smoke and topples over sideways. [Source: Dennis Barnham, *One Man's Window*, p. 62]

Barnham's moment of triumph was brief. Soon after, he ran into more 109s, one of which eventually hit his Spitfire in the engine. Unlike the Germans he did not have to limp home across the sea to Sicily and was able to crash-land at Hal Far, but he was followed down by 109s who sprayed him with machine gun fire. He was taken briefly to the sick quarters and then back to Luqa. Other pilots, of course, were not so lucky. That day Barnham's CO, John Bisdee, was shot down and killed.

The RAF undoubtedly put up a splendid rearguard action against the Luftwaffe, but, as earlier in the year, it was upon the anti-aircraft artillery that the brunt of the defence of Malta fell. By the end of the month they had destroyed 102 enemy aircraft – thirty of those were accounted for in the first week. A Junkers' crew member, interviewed on a German radio programme, described Malta as 'one huge battery of anti-aircraft guns'. He went on to say that: 'the gunners shoot well and the German aircraft need the highest skill and courage to get through.'

Of course this success was only achieved at the cost of a heavy

May 1942: Dobbie Replaced by Lord Gort

expenditure of ammunition. By 20 April there was only slightly over a month's supply remaining, and consumption had to be rationed to fifteen rounds a gun, except for special occasions, such as the arrival of the Spitfires. The shortage of ammunition presented Dobbie with a difficult dilemma: on the one hand, conserving ammunition meant the bombers could not be kept away from the dockyards and the aerodromes; on the other hand, if the ammunition was used up, the AA would be unable to protect the arrival of a fresh convoy, which was urgently needed. A short term solution was the creation of a 'sanctuary' at Ta' Qali, where fighters could return to if they were damaged or had run out of ammunition. Here the Bofors guns were not limited in the number of rounds they could fire.

May 1942: Dobbie Replaced by Lord Gort

As the air battle reaches its climax, Malta is surprised by the sudden announcement that General Lord Gort has succeeded Sir William Dobbie as Governor and Commander-in-Chief of the island.

The new batch of Spitfires, which arrived on 9 May, made all the difference and enabled the RAF to regain control of the skies over Malta. However, just as significant was the change in German tactics. Kesselring was convinced that Malta had been effectively neutralized and the decision was taken that forty-five fighters and forty-five dive bombers were to be transferred to North Africa, while a bomber and fighter group was to be sent to Russia. By 28 April there was a marked decrease in raids and increasingly formations of Italian bombers were spotted over Malta.

The lessons drawn from the fate of the first batch of Spitfires, which had been flown in from the *Wasp* had been learnt. Five experienced pilots were sent back to Gibraltar to lead the new squadrons of Spitfires, and meticulous plans were made for their reception. They were to be divided into three groups. The first group would be already airborne before the other two arrived, so that it would be able to give them cover. Each aircraft was numbered, and when it touched down, it would be directed to the corresponding blast pen. There, to quote a description by Colonel Westropp: 'the pilot would get out and at once be given a cup of tea and a sandwich. Meanwhile RAF men would fall upon the plane and see that it was in order, whilst the soldiers filled its tanks and performed any other duties, which were necessary.' Communications between the widely dispersed pens were maintained by Army wireless sets, dispatch riders and signalmen. The AA guns were allowed a generous ration of ammunition. Each plane was to be ready to take off within half an hour of landing. The plane nearest to Westropp took off in 15 minutes, while some planes were ready within six minutes.

All but five of the sixty-four Spitfires arrived safely. Twenty-three landed at Ta' Qali and the other thirty-six went to Luqa and Hal Far. The German counter-attack materialized immediately, and there were altogether nine raids that day. Hal Far was temporarily put out of action, but the Germans managed to destroy only four Spitfires.

Meanwhile, on 8 May HMS *Welshman*, carrying 340 tons of stores – mostly ammunition and smoke generators – had left Gibraltar disguised as a large French destroyer. Although at one juncture she was carefully examined by two Ju 88s, she reached Malta at 5.25am on the 10th. At 5.54am German aircraft made a reconnaissance of the harbour area. An hour later, unloading – supervised by the naval working parties and carried out by troops – had begun. But at 10am German raiders returned to carry out bombing attacks.

The heaviest raid of the day came at 10.56am, when twenty Stukas and ten Ju 88s, escorted by Me 109s, dropped some 40 tons of bombs on the harbour area. These were met by a force of thirty-seven Spitfires and thirteen Hurricanes. For the first time in Malta a smoke screen was fired over the harbour. An expert to advise on this had been flown in on 1 May, and a small number of smoke generators reached the island by submarine. A gun barrage had also been specially prepared to cover the *Welshman*, and again, all restrictions on ammunition expenditure were lifted.

There were more attacks throughout the day, but each time the RAF was able to counter them with equal or superior forces. Some sixty-five Axis aircraft were lost or damaged in the day's fighting, while the RAF lost just four. At 8.40pm the *Welshman* was able to slip out of harbour for her return voyage to Gibraltar. By 18 May it was clear the RAF had again established local air superiority.

*   *   *

May 1942: Dobbie Replaced by Lord Gort

Both in Britain and in Malta the general impression was that Sir William Dobbie was doing an excellent job. He was an intensely dutiful man and a convinced Christian, who attempted to ensure the Colonial Office and British Government treated the Maltese as fairly as possible. He was certainly liked and respected by the Maltese, and was very aware of ensuring their support for the Government. But he was an object of considerable criticism from the *Times of Malta*. Its editor, Mabel Strickland, had already criticized him for the Government's tardiness in the clean-up operations after the HMS *Illustrious* 'blitz'. She was also convinced that he was a defeatist at heart, who would surrender the island to the Germans: a view she had shared with Mountbatten. Over a year later she was even more adamant he should go. There was no evidence to support the view that Dobbie was a defeatist, but he was a realist, and in early spring 1942 he did not disguise the parlous situation in which Malta found itself. Few would disagree with his analysis, made on 20 April, that: 'if Malta is to be held, drastic action is needed now. It is a question of survival'.

It was precisely within this context that Dobbie's style of leadership came under increasing criticism. The tardy unloading of Convoy MW-10 had been a disaster, as had been the destruction of the first batch of *Wasp* Spitfires. The immediate blame for these debacles lay at the door of Admiral Leatham and Air Vice Marshal Lloyd, but as Chairman of the island's Administrative Council and Commander-in-Chief, Dobbie should have intervened and insisted on effective action and plans. Basically Dobbie had become an ineffective chairman and each service chief was going his own way. Meanwhile, Lieutenant Governor Sir Edward Jackson was increasingly making decisions without consulting his boss. In short, Dobbie was exhausted mentally by his responsibilities of the last two years.

In February he had complained to the War Office that he had been trying to function as: 'C-in-C and fortress commander without any staff beyond my AMS [Assistant Military Secretary] except what I have been able to borrow from time to time'. Dobbie lacked sufficient staff to liaise with the Services effectively. He requested the appointment of a full-time staff officer to assist him. The Chiefs of Staff recommended that Malta be put under the ultimate command of HQ Middle East, so that in military matters the three service heads would receive their orders from Cairo, but the Colonial Office feared this would damage the Governor's prestige in the eyes of the Maltese. In the end Dobbie continued as Governor and Commander-in-Chief, except that his orders now came from Cairo rather than the War Office. Significantly, as late as 3 March, the War Office was still able to stress: 'we want to make it clear to you beyond all reasonable doubt that nothing is further from our minds than lack of confidence in you.'

However, on 12 and 13 April Lord Monckton, the acting Minister of State, and Tedder, the AOC Middle East, visited Malta to assess the situation. There they heard the unanimous opinion from all three service commanders and the Lieutenant Governor that Dobbie: 'had lost his grip of the situation and [was] no longer capable of affording the higher direction and control which must come from an effective Governor'. Consequently they recommended his speedy replacement 'by a leader who would take a more firm grip on the situation'. They did not believe this would in any way demoralize the Maltese, who would, on the contrary, respond to a more dynamic leadership.

Churchill received this recommendation a week later and referred the matter to the Chiefs of Staff. Lord Cranborne, the Colonial Minister, expressed complete surprise to the unexpectedly negative reports on Dobbie, and stressed that he had: 'every reason to suppose that he was doing admirably, and was in fact the life and soul of the defence of Malta'. He also pointed out that Dobbie had been played up as a great national hero. Consequently he feared his dismissal would have a negative impact on public opinion in both Malta and the UK. Meanwhile, Dobbie made it quite clear he would go with good grace, but he was stung by reading a telegram on 21 April from Mabel Strickland to Lord Mountbatten, urging his removal, as he was 'the man responsible for the disaster to the last convoy'. To Dobbie this was mere backstairs intrigue.

Churchill reacted to this by sending out Richard Casey, the Minister of State for the Middle East, to review the situation. To Monckton and the Defence Committee, Middle East, this appeared to be an inexcusable prevarication that merely delayed the chance of implementing changes that might lead to 'some coordination of control' as well as apparently showing that Churchill had little confidence in their judgement. Casey reached Malta on 1 May and after further consultation came to the conclusion that:

An 'Ironside of a man', Major General Sir William Dobbie replaced General Sir Charles Bonham-Carter as Malta's Acting Governor in April 1940.

Sir Andrew Cunningham, Commander-in-Chief of the British Mediterranean Fleet.

Churchill predicted the besieged Maltese would 'make the defence glorious in British military history, and also in the history of Malta itself.'

Lord Gort replaced Sir William Dobbie as Governor of Malta in May 1942.

Hitler and Mussolini signed the Pact of Steel on 22 May 1939, forming an 'Axis' - a term coined by Mussolini - based on mutual military interests.

Albert Kesselring (1885-1960), leader of Luftflotte II 1940-42 and thereafter Hitler's Commander-in-Chief South.

Erwin Rommel (1891-1944), leader of Germany's legendary Afrikakorps.

A view across Dock Creek from St Michael's Bastion showing the extent of bomb damage.
(C.A. Rowntree)

Grand Harbour at Valletta in October 2004, now empty of warships and given over predominantly to tourism.

A Malta Spitfire serviced by ground crew.

The Junkers 88 (right) and 87 (below) were to prove highly effective in Malta.

Heinkel 111 bombers were relatively easy targets for Spitfires and Hurricanes, but developed a specialized role as torpedo bombers, which they carried out against the Malta convoys.

Messerschmitt 109s - the Luftwaffe's principal fighter aircraft. Only Spitfires could oppose these effectively.

AA battery, Valletta's Grand Harbour.

Valletta's Grand Harbour under aerial bombardment.

'The Morning After', Kingsway, Valletta.

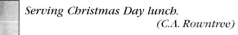
Serving Christmas Day lunch.
(C.A. Rowntree)

Bomb damage: Valletta.
(Louis Henwood)

A Victory kitchen queue.
(C.A. Rowntree)

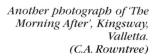

Another photograph of 'The Morning After', Kingsway, Valletta.
(C.A. Rowntree)

After service in the Russian convoys in 1941-2, HMS Speedy *was transferred to the Mediterranean, where she worked as one of the Malta Escort Force for the* Harpoon *and* Pedestal *convoys in June and August 1942.*

The Ohio *before repeated attacks reduced it to a bulk. The ship became the symbol of Operation* Pedestal *or the Santa Marija convoy.*

The aircraft carrier HMS Eagle played a key role in providing Malta with essential Spitfires.

The Brisbane Star, *a survivor of the* Pedestal *convoy, creeps into harbour at Valletta.*
(Edmund Baines' Collection)

Welcoming the Port Chalmers, *a* Pedestal *survivor.* *(Edmund Baines' Collection)*

Another Pedestal *survivor makes port: the* Melbourne Star. *(Edmund Baines' Collection)*

Arrival of the Ohio *at the Grand Harbour.* *(Edmund Baines' Collection)*

Arrival of the Rochester Castle *at the Grand Harbour.* *(Edmund Baines' Collection)*

Onlookers wait for the Ohio *to dock at Valletta.* (Edmund Baines' Collection)

Survivors of the Pedestal *convoy arrive at Valletta.*
(Edmund Baines' Collection)

Grim souvenirs: British submariners engraved victims' names on torpedo forks. One inscription reads:'14th May 1941, HMS Unbeaten/1100 Ton Schooner.'

(Peter Norman)

The George Cross, awarded to the island of Malta for 'supreme gallantry' on 13 September 1942 .

(Tim Addis)

May 1942: Dobbie Replaced by Lord Gort

Dobbie is a man of courage and high character [. . .] But the team here are not working together and the main reason is that Dobbie is no longer capable of vigorous leadership. He has little grasp of [the] situation or power of decision and lacks the knowledge and drive which would enable him to guide and where necessary impose his will. Although respected by the civil population, he is not giving them adequate lead and has failed to get anything like the maximum out of them. For example with the population of 300,000 it should have been possible to organize [a] large body of adult male labourers to work under discipline in support services. Accomplishment in this field has been totally inadequate. Situation today is regrettable. It would become a menace if shortage food or threat of invasion put [the] population under further strain. Dobbie's departure will be regretted by [the] people of Malta, but his own view [with] which I agree is that it will be no more than 9 days wonder. [Source: PRO Prem 3/266]

Casey found that the cooperation between the service commanders was good but that they had no faith in Sir Edward Jackson. However, he recommended that nothing should be done about him until the arrival of Dobbie's replacement. To the Colonial Office this lack of confidence was again a bombshell, as it had heard previously nothing but good about Jackson. One official warned that 'too strong a hand' in the initial stages of the new governorship 'might have precisely the opposite results from those which it is desired to achieve'.

Dobbie was to be succeeded by Lord Gort, the Governor of Gibraltar and former Commander-in-Chief of the BEF in France, 1939–40. It was planned that he should arrive in Malta on 7 May by flying boat, which would then take Dobbie back to Gibraltar. But the timing of the announcement of Dobbie's resignation to the Maltese people presented a problem. Cranborne feared a leak to Madrid across the Gibraltar frontier, 'which would be meat and drink to Axis propagandists who will put the worst interpretation on it'. Meanwhile, Dobbie pointed out that the Maltese would be all too aware of the preparations for his departure and that it seemed: 'hardly fair to the people that they should be left without any announcement or explanation of a change of governor, of which they

will certainly have become aware'. And adding that, as a consequence, 'all sorts of wild speculations will be current'.

Churchill was, however, adamant the announcement should first be
made in Parliament and then to the Maltese on the Rediffusion
system. The pill was to be sweetened by stressing at every opportunity
that Gort had won the VC in the First World War and that he had
brought with him the George Cross for the whole island (see p.117).

What problems with the civilian population and administration did
Gort encounter? Between January and the end of April 1942 over
700 people were killed and 1,000 hospitalized. Some 4,350 buildings
were completely destroyed, while 4,300 were badly damaged. All in
all, about 55 per cent of the populated areas had been destroyed by
early May. The Luftwaffe's main targets, as a year earlier, were the
Grand Harbour, and the three aerodromes, Luqa (with the Safi
Strip), Ta' Qali and Hal Far. Andrew Acheson, a Colonial Office
official who visited Malta in June, reported that the dockyard had
ceased to exist, describing it as: 'a mere heap of stones and twisted
metal'. And yet he added that 'a certain amount of work' was going
on in underground workshops. He also observed that the destruction
in the Three Cities was almost as complete, and that he had not seen
anything to compare with it, 'except certain cities on the Western
Front during the last war'.

Although the towns and villages away from this area were safer,
they were not immune to attack, as the Luftwaffe controlled the skies
above Malta until the arrival of the second *Wasp* cargo of Spitfires on
9 May, and could strike where it wished. The Police Air Raid Reports
regularly reported a depressing catalogue of destruction. In Zetjun,
for instance, on 2 May, a bomb was dropped on the main square
killing twenty-one people and injuring a further twenty-nine, while
another bomb hit a wing of St Paul's Home for the Old at Hamrun,
killing thirty-seven patients and one nurse.

The key factor in maintaining morale during those terrible months
was the existence of the deep shelters. By January 1942 about 20
miles of tunnel, averaging a little over 6 x 6 feet in size, existed and
more were constructed in the following months. The largest was
about 1 mile long and was fitted with beds and deck chairs. Gunner
Fleming was impressed by the lack of immorality in the shelters,

May 1942: Dobbie Replaced by Lord Gort

which he put down to the deep rooted Catholicism of the Maltese. He noted that in all the shelters there were small altars and figures of Christ or the Virgin Mary with flowers and candles placed around them. He recalled later that he had 'often walked through the tunnel – both early morning and evening – and seen women in bed and at various stage of dressing – yet no one took any notice'.

Once the siren sounded, inevitably most people sought safety in the air raid shelters and tunnels, regardless of whether the raid was actually targeting their vicinity or not. As the average period of a raid lengthened, the red flag system was introduced in Valletta and the surrounding area, in an attempt to minimize the disruption caused by a raid. As soon as there was a danger of bombing in the harbour area, a red flag was hoisted on the Palace and the Castille to warn people to take cover. Once it became clear the Germans were targeting another area, the flag was lowered. Norah Goreing remembered the horror of these moments:

> 'Run!' said dad when he saw the warning flag being hurriedly raised on the look-out tower at Castille Palace [. . .] Then came the whirling rise and fall of air raid sirens giving the stomach-churning warning. Masses of people running in all directions towards the shelters. We ran as fast as our legs could carry us towards cover, passing soldiers, who had released the smoke screen, we reached the shelter and the soldiers close behind. Gunfire rumbled with increasing intensity. The dive bombers were screaming down seemingly from every direction, bombs crashing down with incredible violence. 'This was it,' I thought, 'nothing could save us now.' A terrible feeling of doom was on us once again. The shelter rocked and trembled with the concussion of explosions and for what seemed like an eternity the whole area went as black as night before the flying debris and dust settled. [Source: Goreing IWM 92/30/1]

The intensity of the blitz inevitably created enormous problems for the Government, as each month there were about 800 houses destroyed. The most immediate problems were the accommodation of thousands of homeless bombed-out people, the breakdown of communications and the difficulties in distributing food. Refugee centres were established both in the bombed-out areas and in the relative safety of the small towns and villages away from Valletta and the airfields. In Senglea, for instance, families built wooden huts to live in, and in Marsa and Luqa the Protection Officers urged families to use material from ruined houses to construct temporary rooms for their families. Thousands, however, fled Valletta and the Three Cities to other areas of the island. By the end of April there were tens of thousands of refugees on the move. In an attempt to impose some degree of order the Government announced that no families or individuals could move from the area of one Protection Officer to another unless they gave notice of their intention. In the South Eastern Region the Protection Officer had no spare accommodation and a goat pen had to be cleaned in order to house thirty people. Elsewhere schools, religious houses and the crypts of churches were used to house refugees. At Civita Vecchia a disused Renaissance convent was turned into a refugee centre. One British official noted that:

> on the first floor of the convent, in what had been the dormitory of the nuns, a big glassed-in loggia looking out on a courtyard, were numbers of two-decker wooden bunks for the immediate reception of refugees from blitzed areas on the model of those which had been set up in London tube stations. [Source: PRO CO 96789]

The continued raids also made the distribution of food to the refugee centres difficult. Food shops were destroyed, telephone communications were disrupted, water pipes and reservoirs damaged and power cut off from bakeries and flower mills. The Government responded by setting up emergency mobile canteens and appointing liaison officers to maintain contact between the Lieutenant Governor's office and the Protection Officers to ensure the effective distribution of bread. Stand pipes were set up in Senglea, and in Valletta Water Works both Engineers and the Royal Engineers laid hundreds of feet of water pipes.

Throughout the blitz of January–May 1942 it was important to keep the administration of the island running as smoothly as possible. Most Government departments were moved out of Valletta, but this only caused more disruption and hardship for the

May 1942: Dobbie Replaced by Lord Gort

employees, who were now faced with dangerous bus journeys. The Rabat terminus near the Ta' Qali aerodrome was, for instance, a very dangerous spot. In mid-March 1942 workers getting off the bus were suddenly caught in a heavy attack. As bombs burst all around, passengers could only throw themselves flat on the ground in an attempt to escape blast and splinters.

Schools and education were also hit hard. Many school buildings were requisitioned by the Government and over 100 male teachers were either called up or transferred full time to civil defence duties. The schools also had to cope with the influx of a large number of evacuees from Valletta and the Three Cities. Teaching was also disrupted by the raids, but when it did take place, it was often in makeshift class rooms without pencils, paper or chalk. Inevitably in this situation, attendance fell. To quote the report by the Senior Inspector of Education in Malta: 'Children who had to spend the greater part of the nights dozing on a small uncomfortable stool in a crowded shelter, could not be drawn out of a cosy bed when it was time to go to school.'

Gort's first impression of the situation in Malta was that there was a 'lack of coordination, lack of forward planning and general lack of harmony'. He informed Middle East High Command that: 'unless everything is pulled together with a firm and vigorous hand the policy of drift must continue towards inevitable disaster.' He was quite clear in his own mind that there was no question of Malta acting as a base for any naval or air offensive until 'the present critical situation' had been corrected. He insisted that if he was to have any chance of providing the necessary leadership to save Malta, he must have it unambiguously confirmed that he was the Supreme Commander in Malta. His original terms of appointment had stressed that the senior service commanders in Malta came under the command of HQ Middle East unless Malta was invaded, when Gort himself would then take over the supreme command. Gort argued that this was a recipe for chaos and insisted that at this 'critical stage the fighting service and the civil administration must operate in Malta under one supreme commander'.

The initial reaction of one Colonial Office representative, W. Rolleston, was to point out that Malta was not yet in the position of

Campaign Chronicle

Corregidor in the Pacific: 'which held out as a gallant gesture in order to contain enemy forces'. On the contrary Malta was only worth retaining for the influence it could bring to bear on general Mediterranean strategy. Thus Rolleston continued:

> To justify the effort of retaining Malta, the island must pay a dividend. No one will try to force Lord Gort into paying that dividend too soon, but that decision on when and how [to use] the island as a base for offensive air and possibly sea action must [. . .] be taken in Cairo.

Richard Casey, the Minister of State at Cairo amended the wording of the appointment to ensure that when, in Gort's judgement, the safety of the island was endangered, he would be able to exercise supreme authority; but this worried Lord Cranborne, the Colonial Secretary, who feared Gort's prestige would suffer if he did not enjoy the same powers as Dobbie and Bonham-Carter before him. He pointed out that: 'Malta is an extremely political colony. Even in these difficult times the political aspects of civil administration constantly tend to intrude themselves, and in various ways political and religious susceptibilities must be given due weight.' Finally, Churchill put an end to further debate by appointing Gort Supreme Commander of the fighting services until further notice.

Gort's first preoccupation was naturally the defence and re-victualling of the island, but he realized the importance of keeping in contact with the Maltese people. According to a Colonial Office report written by Acheson in July: 'Day after day in sweltering heat, he bicycles to save petrol – through their towns and villages, and he speaks to everyone he meets, and I was immensely stuck by the genuine affection with which he was everywhere greeted.' Gort also led by example, taking 'immense pains to deny himself everything that is denied to others', thus there was neither hot water nor electric light in Government House.

But for all his emphasis on harmony, Gort was not good at dealing with civilian administrators or Maltese politicians. At Government House, which exuded the atmosphere of an army headquarters in the field, Gort surrounded himself with a large staff of military, naval and RAF officers. General Beckett, who was in charge of the anti-aircraft defences, welcomed the new regime. Under Dobbie he felt that he had 'as many masters as there days of the week' to cope with, but now with Gort 'in full command' the chaos was being sorted out. Acheson, however, formed the opinion that Gort not only found it hard to get along with civilian bureaucrats, but actually despised them. Consequently, Gort saw relatively little of his Lieutenant Governor, Sir William Jackson, and some of the other officials.

The problem was compounded by the fact that the coordinating committee, which acted as a liaison between the service chiefs and the civilian administration, was chaired by Captain Guy Russell RN, another service official dismissive of civilians. The upshot of this was that, far from there being friendly and harmonious relations in beleaguered fortress Malta, there was a considerable attitude of strain and mutual suspicion. This was seen in the attitude of Sir Edward Jackson, who was bewildered and resentful at his treatment by Gort. According to Acheson: 'each thought the other was trying to act behind his back.'

June 1942: Reduced Rations

With the running of convoys still a perilous operation, the supply situation on Malta continues to deteriorate. Rations are reduced still further and morale becomes increasingly brittle.

On 4 April the Admiralty announced that it could not run another convoy through to Malta from either the east or the west until the fighter force on the island had been strongly reinforced. The destruction of the majority of the forty-seven Spitfires, which landed on Malta from the *Wasp* on 20 April also persuaded the Chiefs of Staff to cancel plans for sending a convoy in May as it could not afford to risk any more of its capital ships and carriers. Instead, priority was given to running Convoy PQ-16 through to Murmansk. This was very bad news for Malta. Consequently, on 5 May, the bread ration was cut by 25 per cent to 10½ ounces a day. Provided the mills were not destroyed, this would enable the Maltese to survive until July.

Soon after his arrival Lord Gort announced a stocktaking of all essential commodities, and within a week cuts were announced in sugar and rice rations, and because of fodder shortages all surplus animals were to be killed.

In June it was decided to attempt to send another convoy to Malta, but to have any chance of success, it was, as the Commander-in-Chief of the Mediterranean Fleet insisted, 'essential to disperse the enemy's effort both on the surface and in the air'. Thus the decision was taken to run two convoys from each end of the Mediterranean: Operation *Harpoon* from the west and *Vigorous* from the east, both of which would be assisted 'by every possible diversion'. To ease the congestion in the Grand Harbour *Harpoon* was to arrive twenty-four hours before *Vigorous*. Crucial to the success of these two convoys was the expected military advance in North Africa, but to quote the Official History: 'Worst of all, instead of the Army advancing [. . .] and capturing the airfields in Cyrenaica, the enemy had struck first, and the passage of the June convoys coincided with the height of the land battle, which was going badly for the British.'

To spare the Navy's dwindling reserve of capital ships, the gamble was taken to limit *Harpoon*'s escort force to cruisers, destroyers, the old battleship, *Malaya* and the carriers, *Eagle* and *Argus*. The actual convoy comprised of five freighters, the British *Burdwan*, *Orari*, *Troilus*, the Dutch *Tanimbar*, the American *Chant*, as well as a fast American tanker, the *Kentucky*. Local air superiority over Malta was to be ensured by the dispatch of a further fifty-nine Spitfires by two trips of the *Eagle*. To ensure there was sufficient AA ammunition and supplies of smoke cover, the *Welshman* was to accompany the *Harpoon* convoy as far as the Narrows and then make a dash for Malta at 25 knots to arrive at dawn on the day the convoy was due. The main covering force would sail as far as the Skerki Channel and then turn for home. From there until the convoy came within range of the Malta Spitfires lay a period of acute danger, when the ships would have to rely on the protection of the anti-aircraft cruiser *Cairo*, nine destroyers and any Beaufighters that were available.

For Operation *Vigorous* it was clear there was no chance of evading discovery by enemy air reconnaissance: the convoy would just have to be fought through. Consequently, the route chosen was the one best suited to the limited fighter protection available. The convoy was particularly vulnerable because it had no carrier accompanying it. It was escorted by only three 6-inch cruisers and eleven destroyers, but their striking power was to be increased by the employment of the

June 1942: Reduced Rations

First and Tenth Submarine Flotillas as close cover to the convoy during its passage across the Central Basin, and by MTBs, which would be towed until contact with the enemy was made.

To disguise the fact that the convoy was being prepared for Malta, the merchant ships were loaded at Alexandria, Port Said, Suez, Haifa and Beirut. In order to confuse the enemy further, and draw his fleet out to sea prematurely so it would be exposed to air attack, a feint was to be made with part of the convoy some twelve hours before the main convoy set sail.

The decoy convoy sailed on 11 June and met up with the main convoy off Alexandria on afternoon of the 13th, but its strength was gradually eroded through a mixture of mechanical defects and enemy bombing. Three merchant ships had to be detached from the main body and sent in to Tobruk and Mersa Matruh. Meanwhile HMS *Erica* and HMS *Primula* also both developed engine trouble. Enemy air attacks came on the afternoon of 14 June once the convoy came out of range of British fighter cover. The MTV *Potaro* was damaged and the *Bhutan* sunk. That evening attacks by Italian E-Boats began, but resulted in no damage.

At 6.45pm the Italian Fleet was spotted by reconnaissance aircraft leaving Taranto. This consisted of two battleships, two 8-inch and two 6-inch cruisers, and twelve destroyers. The hope was that British air and submarine attacks would force the Italians to retire, but although one heavy cruiser was damaged, the Fleet was not slowed down, and it was clear that it would cross the convoy's path by dawn. Consequently Rear Admiral Vian was ordered to do a U-turn at 2am on the 15th to avoid contact. Just as this complex manoeuvre was completed German E-Boats and a submarine torpedoed the *Newcastle* and sank the destroyer, *Hasty*. Throughout the day further avoidance action took place, but at the cost of making the convoy vulnerable to repeated air attacks in the 'Bomb Alley' between Crete and Cyrenaica. The *Birmingham* and the *Centurion* were both badly damaged and the *Airedale* sunk. A final attempt to race the convoy through to Malta was called off because the escorts were rapidly running out of ammunition, and what was left of the convoy returned to Alexandria.

Harpoon was more successful but at a terrible cost. It was heavily attacked on the morning of 15 June, first by Italian planes based on

Campaign Chronicle

Sardinia and Ju 88s from Sicily. The *Tanimbar* was sunk and the *Liverpool* was hit in the engine room and had to be towed back to Gibraltar. Then, as the convoy steamed by Cape Bon and set course eastwards for Malta, it was ambushed at 6.40am by an Italian force of three 6-inch cruisers and five destroyers. The Italians showed a high standard of gunnery and hit both the *Bedouin* and *Partridge*, but it was the German bombers, which arrived during the naval battle, that did the most damage, sinking the *Chant* and disabling the tanker, *Kentucky*. The Italian Admiral de Zara, discouraged by a dense smoke screen over the convoy, retired northwards, but at 11.20am another air attack was launched and the merchantman, *Burdwan* was disabled. Captain Hardy had little option but to press on to Malta with the two remaining merchantmen, the *Troilus* and the *Orari*, while sinking the two disabled ships, *Kentucky* and *Burdwan*. These did reach Malta, but in the approach to the Grand Harbour, five destroyers strayed into a mine field. The Polish *Kujawiak* sank but the others managed to reach harbour. The *Welshman* arrived first at 7.30am on 15 June and had unloaded all her stores by 1.30pm. Later that afternoon the *Orari* and *Troilus* berthed.

Unloading began immediately and proceeded continuously by day and night. A force of 2,300 Maltese dockers and British servicemen worked in shifts and provided the stevedores, lighter parties, dock-side workers, tally clerks, telephonists and the gangs who loaded the lorries bound for the dispersal dumps. In the event of a heavy air raid warning the working parties were to be sent to shelters ashore, the lorries near the ships were dispersed, and a smoke screen was put over the harbour. Overall less than four hours were lost in this way during the five days and four nights of the unloading. Altogether 15,000 tons of aviation fuel, food and stores were unloaded safely.

Just two merchantmen out of a total of seventeen managed to reach Malta. The C-in-C Mediterranean immediately accepted that another convoy would have to sail, but given that the last three convoys had been a failure, it was only understandable that the Navy was somewhat defeatist about future prospects. Rear Admiral Vian was emphatic that: 'a convoy could not, repetition not, be passed successfully to Malta from the east.' Meanwhile, the C-in-C Mediterranean, Sir Henry Harwood, himself also observed that

June 1942: Reduced Rations

everybody 'naturally has the desire to help Malta, but the trouble is the feeling of impossibility. This is based on the failure of the last three convoys.'

On the island there had been exaggerated hopes that at a stroke the convoy would break the Siege of Malta. Airman Rogers and his friends had daydreams of it miraculously arriving intact and inaugurating a new era when there would be 'big eats and beer in the café's [*sic*], again – soap, tooth paste, toilet paper . . .' The reality, of course, was different. Air Vice Marshal Lloyd witnessed the arrival of the two survivors:

> Thousands of people watched the two ships, *Troilus* and *Orari* enter the Grand Harbour late in the afternoon of the 15th. Both were battered and damaged. There was scarcely a cheer; it was victory sure enough but it was more of an occasion for deep reverence than for joy [. . .] As I looked down at those ships coming up the harbour they reminded me of two lone survivors of a band of warriors returning triumphantly from battle, covered with blood and scars and so fatigued as to be scarcely able to put one foot in front of the other. [Source: quoted in J. Douglas-Hamilton, *The Air Battle for Malta*, p. 77]

There was, too, a feeling of guilt at the human cost of the convoy. Rogers summed this up when he later observed that: 'we are eating, but only at the expense of men's' lives – they died for us in their hundreds.' He also bitterly asked: 'how many loaves of bread equal a man's life?'

Despite the arrival of the two ships, the daily ration actually declined, but, as General Westropp succinctly put it: 'without their arrival the island would probably not have been able to hold out until August'. On the 16th Gort broadcast to the island:

> I must break to you what the arrival of only two ships means to us. For some time past we have been short of supplies and further privations lie ahead of us [. . .] We must stand on our resources and everyone of us must do everything in his or her power to conserve stocks and to ensure that best use of all the

available resources remain to us [. . .] we must make all possible savings in every commodity and stock.

The crucial thing was to try to make an accurate inventory of present stocks, assess how long they would last and work out the scale of rations accordingly. The target date was at first set for mid-October. Two British officials from the Ministry of Food in London worked out the following figures for the Maltese population as a whole:

	Pre-War Monthly Consumption	Consumption Before June Convoy	Level To Which Consumption Had To Be Reduced To Make Stocks Last Until October
	In Tons Except For Milk		
Flour	3000	2000	2000
Edible Oil	165	135	45
Sugar	750	240	180
Lard/Margarine	119	93	93
Butter	36	15	(Included in Above)
Cheese	60	37.5	20
Coffee	64	51	(Minimal)
Tea	15	14	14
Canned Meat/Fish	Not Known	150	200
Rice	63	72	18
Milk	7800 Cases	6000 Cases	6000 Cases

(Source: J. Micallef, *When Malta Stood Alone*, p. 166)

In July these figures were questioned by another British official, Alaric Rowntree, who argued that they were based on 'very suspect figures of pre-war consumption', and that actually they gave rather an optimistic assessment of the situation! However, the new ration scale was announced on 20 June, which involved lowering the average daily per capita calories for the Maltese still further. In 1939/40 it had been 2,500. Now it was less than 1,500. It was vital, if Malta was to survive, to persuade the farmers to surrender their cereal crops to state controlled mills so that they could be distributed to the whole population. The Government was ready to buy grain at a reasonably generous price, but there were angry demonstrations

June 1942: Reduced Rations

when the policy was announced on 21 July. The Government had little option but to start requisitioning cereals, leaving only enough for seed corn. Collection centres were set up in the villages and farmers were paid cash on the spot. In August Lord Gort complained that: 'the collection of grain [had fallen] off very seriously'. This was partly a result of the poor harvest, but it was also caused by hoarding. In some villages the local priest played a key role in persuading the farmers to hand over grain to the authorities.

The farmers were also encouraged to kill off their surplus live-stock, as there was an acute shortage of imported fodder. Between 3 July and 26 September over 12,000 sheep and goats were killed and their carcasses sold to the Government, which then redistributed them to the communal kitchens and retailers at a special subsidized rate. Steps were also taken to compel private individuals to declare how much food they had in reserve. Initially, at any rate, these stocks would not be compulsorily purchased, but there was considerable hostility to filling in the stocktaking returns.

In the first six months of 1942 the system of communal kitchens or 'Victory Kitchens', as they were renamed, was expanded to cover the whole of Malta, which was divided into eight districts, each controlled by an Area Manager. Their original purpose had been to cater for the refugees, but increasingly as the blockade bit, more and more Maltese made use of them. They were not popular and frequently criticized, but in December 1942 they were given grudging praise by Mabel Strickland in the *Times of Malta*: 'The Siege Kitchens of Malta provided the means by which all were hungry together but nobody starved outright.'

Thanks to effective preventative steps taken, officials from the Ministry of Health in Britain were able to confirm in July 1942 that: 'up to the present the health situation in Malta compared favourably with the UK, save in infant mortality.' This was partly the result of the forethought of Professor Bernard, the Principal Medical Officer in Malta, who introduced a system of medical and sanitary surveillance for dormitory shelters and refugee centres. Medical inspections took place daily, and no new entrants were allowed into shelters without medical inspection. Diphtheria was also controlled through immunization. The officials from the Ministry of Health were also impressed by how it had been possible to provide working places within the shelters 'where the shelterers can clean their bedding and personal belongings'. But owing to malnutrition and the shortage of soap, scabies – particularly amongst the children – 'spread like a forest fire' to quote the Chief Education Officer, proving to be 'an enemy more powerful than the Hun . . .'

By June 1942 the main threat to the Maltese was starvation rather than bombs. Colonel Dixon of the RAMC, in a lecture on Maltese medical facilities, remarked that:

> homage and credit has been given to the Maltese garrison and the people for standing up to bombing. I am not sure that sufficient homage and credit has been given for standing up to starvation. It is bad enough to be bombed to blazes, but to be hungry at the same time is Hell! [Source: WO222/239]

British servicemen received slightly better rations than the Maltese, but that did not stop them feeling constantly hungry. The Army introduced a breadless day once a week, and for the rest of the time rations consisted of hard Army biscuit, tinned beef, tea and condensed milk. The Navy, too, had progressively to cut down its rations. In May rations of frozen meat, milk, sugar and potatoes were all drastically cut. The rules covering the consumption of bread were so tight that an attempt to issue the crew of the *Ploughboy* with an extra pound of bread between four people, when they went out mine sweeping, led to bitter reprimands and the demand for a letter of explanation. In response to the accusation that he was acting in a petty manner the Superintendent of the Victualling yard insisted he had strict orders from Vice Admiral Leatham to check each item of rations issued.

Gort was also very anxious compulsorily to evacuate all service families and civilians who were not doing essential work. He particularly wanted to dispatch those who were suffering from nervous breakdowns, diabetes or tuberculosis and 'a troup of variety artists', but in June 1942 the War Cabinet specifically decided that evacuations should cease, both because of the difficulty of transport and out of regard to the impact on Maltese morale.

It was, of course, not just starvation that faced the Maltese. Shortages affected every part of their life. It was, for instance, a constant source of worry for the Government whether it would be able to maintain sufficient bank notes in circulation, and plans had to be made either to fly in or send by submarine regular supplies. Clothes too were a problem. The longer the siege lasted, the more resourceful the garrison and the inhabitants had to be in cobbling together sufficient clothes and shoes to wear. Nora Goreing's family used the padding from smoke screen containers for their shoes, while increasingly the uniform of the service personnel became more and more casual. Rogers, for example observed that: 'our modern re-vamped airman now looks a bit of a sight with his [. . .] assorted dress, filthy buttons and bristly chin, long hair, an assortment of bites, spots and open sores on his body, which by now is getting scarce on flesh.'

All reports coming from Malta stressed that while the morale of the Maltese was still good, it was becoming increasingly 'brittle'. Gort summed up the mood in a letter to Cranborne on 7 July:

> Despite their straightened circumstances the morale of the population remains good but it is undeniably brittle and I can detect a tendency for criticism to increase. One has to realize that the people took the reverses in Libya badly as they always feel that our future is bound up with events in Egypt. Unfortunately these reverses followed closely on the failure of the convoy and the additional food and other restrictions I had to impose as a consequence. [Source: PRO CO 967/89]

Acheson, on his visit to the island in July, was told that: 'in the week after the fall of Tobruk not a smile was seen on the island.' He warned Cranborne that although the Maltese 'are passionately loyal [. . .] they are shaken, and should another convoy fail to reach them, their morale may very easily crack, suddenly and catastrophically.' This is why Gort was so anxious that the Colonial Secretary himself should visit Malta to show that the island had not been forgotten.

When Cranborne did arrive in early August, Gort stressed it was important that the suffering the Maltese people were enduring should be recognized in Britain. To record the siege he had already set up a Historical Branch and he also wanted the appointment of a full-time information officer.

Campaign Chronicle

July 1942: Allied Air Superiority Established

*The number of German air raids increase in
anticipation of the dispatch of another convoy.
Meanwhile, given the desperate struggle in North
Africa, Malta is increasingly being used as a staging
post for aircraft en route to Egypt and again as a base
for operations against Axis supply lines.*

Although there were repeated attacks against *Harpoon* and
Vigorous, enemy air activity over Malta in June was relatively slight.
For the first two weeks in July, however, there were sixty-five Axis
attacks on the aerodromes, which resulted in thirty-four planes on

---

Sir Keith Park's 'Forward Plan of Fighter Protection'

Given that the RAF in Malta now had approximately the
same number or even more fighters than the Axis, Park
introduced what he called 'a simple fighter plan for intercepting the enemy raids north of Malta before they could cross
the coast and bomb our aerodromes'. In essence it involved
three or four squadrons under the control of the Fighter Sector
Controller gaining the necessary height 'up sun'. The first two
squadrons attacked the escorting fighters, while the third and
fourth concentrated on the bombers. Previously it had been left
to the fighters to decide for themselves where to patrol and
when to intercept the enemy. Park stressed that the Controller
'cannot win an air combat in a hundred years, but he can lose
a combat in a hundred seconds'. His job was to anticipate the
enemy's movements and then place the fighters in the best
possible position to intercept the enemy according to the position of the sun and clouds. Above all, he had to work out time
and distance calculations at high speed.

To ensure this new plan worked effectively, Park managed to
obtain from the UK new radar equipment and 'scientific
officers' who could advise on its operation. As most of the

---

the ground being put out of operation, a number of causalities among the RAF, Army and civilian personnel, and a considerable amount of damage to runways, perimeter tracks and roads. On 14 July Air Vice Marshal Lloyd was replaced by Sir Keith Park, who had commanded No. 11 Group in the Battle of Britain. To avoid a repetition of this damage Park introduced a new 'Forward Plan of Fighter Protection'.

Park's new tactics, assisted by the fact that the bulk of the Luftwaffe had been recalled to Egypt and Russia, certainly helped minimize the impact of Axis raids on Malta in late July, which was a relatively quiet time – by Maltese standards. However, Gort did warn

fighting would now take place over the sea, he increased the sea rescue service by borrowing a high speed launch from the Army and arranging for the Air Ministry to send out several more RAF launches. He pointedly stressed that 'the enemy attacking Malta has to fly a long way from his own sea rescue service and friendly territory.' Park also tightened up on wireless discipline and banned 'unnecessary messages' and 'chatter'. He argued that intercepting the enemy before they reached the target had several clear advantages:

- It would reduce casualties and damage to airfields if the enemy bombers had to jettison their bombs over the sea.
- Radar worked more effectively when the enemy was approaching and their formations had not become intermingled with the British planes.
- Bombers were more vulnerable when approaching their target. Once they had dropped their bombs they were free to take intricate evasive tactics.
- British planes would have fuller fuel tanks and more ammunition if they initially intercepted enemy fighters over the sea, rather than pursuing them after a raid had taken place.

Campaign Chronicle

Cranborne against complacency when he stressed that the Germans had always been able to bring back enough bombers at short notice to attack a convoy, as they had 'brought the mobility of aircraft to a high standard due to the ease of maintenance through concentrating on a few efficient types'. A few days later, on 22 July, Alaric Rowntree, the nutritional expert from Britain arrived on the island, noted in his diary that: 'the raids continue as usual, in fact one does not really know when one is on or not, they are so frequent.'

With the re-establishment of British air superiority over Malta and the desperate situation in North Africa, Malta was once again becoming a vital base from which both submarines and aircraft could strike at Axis shipping en route for Tripoli. The Tenth Submarine Flotilla was re-established at Lazzaretto. Gort, however, was worried that Malta's offensive role would conflict with his primary task of defending the island by using up scarce fuel. He argued that it was of 'paramount importance' to maintain sufficient Spitfires and fuel to defend Malta. He feared that a repetition of the spring blitz could easily bring Malta to its knees. On 29 July he informed the Chiefs of Staff Middle East that: 'as I see it the choice lies between the continuance of strikes irrespective of over-expenditure of fuel, or the restriction of flying to our daily fighter effort until the arrival and unloading of a convoy.' Until he received firm guidance from HQ Middle East he took the decision as C-in-C Malta to suspend any further long-range strikes from the island. The response from HQ Middle East was to reassure Gort that air units based on Malta would only be authorized to undertake attacks on those targets that 'affected vitally the issue in the Western Desert'. The real solution, of course, lay in the safe arrival of another convoy.

August 1942: Operation *Pedestal*

Pedestal is the make or break attempt to relieve Malta.
If it fails, the island will fall.

The June convoy had bought a few weeks for Malta, but further supplies were needed by August at the latest if the island was to survive. It is true that a constant trickle of supplies through the 'magic carpet', or in other words in submarines, did manage to get

August 1942: Operation *Pedestal*

Onboard an American Merchantman

In each merchant ship there were naval liaison officers. In the mess of the American merchantman, the *Almeira*, the Captain decided to sit the two British officers at a separate table, 'as he was afraid that some of his crew were not very pro British'. One of them, Lieutenant Commander Marshall, was somewhat sceptical about the crew's intention of putting in a demand for extra pay on the grounds that they were not getting proper food, as 'they could not have four eggs for breakfast'!

through. Although the Americans were unwilling to loan any of their large submarines, as they were needed in the Pacific, two British submarines, the *Olympus* and the *Clyde* were modified to carry stores, particularly Bofors' spares, medicine and kerosene to Malta, but this, at most, added up to a mere trickle.

On 15 June – that is the same day as just two merchant ships out of the seventeen sailing with *Harpoon* and *Vigorous* limped into the Grand Harbour – the Chiefs of Staff approved, in principle, a further convoy to be run to Malta from the west. It was accepted that to sail from the east was suicidal. This decision was made possible by the Battle of Midway, the American naval victory over the Japanese forces in the Pacific (which ensured there was now no longer pressure for British naval units to move to the Far East), and by the suspension of the Arctic convoys to the USSR until the autumn.

Detailed planning of the Malta convoy began on 29 July in London. Learning from *Harpoon*'s relative failure, it was decided that *Pedestal* needed much heavier air cover between the south of Sardinia and the mouth of the Narrows. It also needed a larger escort of cruisers and destroyers for it to complete safely the final stage of the voyage through the Sicilian Channel to Malta. A formidable force under Admiral Syfret was assembled, comprising: two battleships, the *Nelson* and the *Rodney*; some seventy-two Fleet Air Arm planes based on the three aircraft carriers, *Victorious*, *Indomitable* and *Eagle*; seven cruisers and twenty-six destroyers. In addition, there were two fleet oilers and a tug, which were to be

101

Campaign Chronicle

escorted by four corvettes and two mine sweepers. This force was to escort eleven large merchantmen and the tanker, the *Ohio*, which was loaned by the Americans. In case the *Ohio* was sunk, the cargoes of the other ships were a balance of cans of petrol and aviation spirit, flour, ammunition and shells.

As with Operation *Harpoon*, the escorts were to be divided into two forces: Force X under Admiral Syfret, which was composed of the battleships, the aircraft carriers and their escorts; and Force Z under Rear Admiral Burrough. The former would turn back to Gibraltar at the Skerki Channel, while the latter would steam on for Malta. Although there was to be no eastern convoy, a dummy convoy would run from Alexandria but turn around on 11 August. Belatedly it was ordered that the Aircraft Carrier *Furious* should be attached to the *Pedestal* convoy and fly off further Spitfire reinforcements to Malta.

On 2 August the loading of the merchantmen on the *Clyde* was finished and the convoy set sail. When Lieutenant Blundell on the *Nelson* first read the orders for the operation, he confessed in the diary that: 'it makes me sweat reading the bit about the poor convoy getting through the last bit . . .'As they steamed down to Gibraltar, where they were to meet up with the aircraft carriers, they were joined by the squadrons of its escorts. Despite frequent alarms there were no successful U-Boat attacks. The convoy was repeatedly exercised in taking emergency turns and changing positions so as to avoid future enemy attacks, eventually reaching – according to Admiral Syfret, who had the overall command of the convoy – 'an efficiency in manoeuvring comparable to that of a Fleet unit'.

Dummy air attacks were also arranged as the convoy approached Gibraltar on 8 August, followed by a fly past of British planes for identification purposes. The convoy passed through the Straits of Gibraltar at 11pm, where it encountered thick fog. It passed one neutral merchant vessel steaming west and a fleet of small Spanish fishing vessels, amongst which it was feared were pro Axis Spanish spies, who would communicate the position of the fleet to the Germans and Italians. So far D1 had been an uneventful day. H.E. Venn, a sailor on the *Indomitable* remembered how he 'laughed, danced and skylarked on the flight deck in the sun'. (IWM 92/27/1) But the following day, 11 August, was not to so peaceful. Initially the

August 1942: Operation *Pedestal*

How much did the Axis Know About Pedestal?

For secrecy's sake the *Pedestal* convoy was given a bogus number, 5.21.S, which indicated that it was sailing to Suez via the Cape. However, it was an open secret that the convoy was sailing to Malta. Charts of the Mediterranean had been issued to the escorting ships, and it seems that even some crates had been loaded onboard marked for Malta. When the convoy commodore, Commander A.G. Venables, joined the *Port Chalmers*, he was even told by the stevedores that the ship was bound for Malta! In response to complaints, voiced in a secret session of the House of Lords on 29 September by Admiral of the Fleet, Lord Cork and Orrery, an enquiry was conducted by the Ministry of War Transport. German records show that some information had certainly reached Admiral Weichold, the German Naval Commander-in-Chief, Mediterranean at the end of July. However, the details of the convoy were communicated to the Axis by German *Abwehr* agents working from a special observation post at Cidilla, on the coast of Algeciras in Spanish Morocco, which enabled them to observe all Allied shipping

re-fuelling of three cruisers and twenty-six destroyers was success-fully completed and the thirty-seven Spitfires on the *Furious* were flown off for Malta, but at 1.15pm the *Eagle* was torpedoed by the German submarine U-73, which had managed to dive undetected beneath the convoy columns. The *Eagle* sank in eight minutes, but fortunately the majority of her crew were rescued. By now the convoy was being continuously shadowed by reconnaissance planes. In the evening it was attacked by thirty-six German bombers and torpedo bombers, but its guns put up an immense barrage and little damage was done. Lieutenant Barton, the Naval Liaison Officer on the *Ohio*, 'had never seen anything so colossal as the barrage the ships put up' and could not believe that any planes could come through it.

The next day, 12 August, saw further sustained air attacks. First, some eighty German and Italian planes attacked in waves, but the convoy had been so well drilled in avoidance measures that, to quote the Official history, its ships 'were manoeuvring together like a squadron of warships'. Near Galita an Italian submarine was rammed so vigorously by HMS *Ithuriel* that she badly damaged herself and put her asdic gear out of action. A boarding party was landed on the submarine but discovered no papers of value. In his report Lieutenant Evans mentioned that: 'there were three or four Italians on top of the conning tower and the hatch was open. One of them was looking at his watch; whether he was timing a scuttling charge or just bemoaning the fact that it was full of salt water I do not know.'

In the afternoon casualties began to mount. First of all the *Deucalion* was damaged and had to be detached under the escort of the *Bramham* to follow an inshore route along the Tunisian coast, where she was later attacked and sunk by two Italian torpedo boats. Then the destroyer *Foresight* was struck by a torpedo from a Savoia and the *Indomitable* received three direct hits that put her flight deck out of action. That evening, as the convoy was approaching the Skerki Channel, Force Z, as planned, turned back to Gibraltar, although the attack on *Indomitable* brought this decision forward by twenty minutes. Admiral Burrough continued with Force X.

Optimistically it was hoped that, given the weight of air attacks during the day, there would be no further attacks until the morning, and that the Skerki banks would provide protection against submarines. But at 8pm an Italian submarine, the *Axum*, caught the fleet at a vulnerable, perhaps even 'chaotic'– to quote the Commanding Officer of the *Kenya* – moment, when it was changing from four columns to two. The consequence was that not only did HMS *Nigeria* and the *Cairo* but also the *Ohio* receive under-water hits. Lieutenant Barton on the *Ohio* was looking at the stricken *Cairo*:

> when there was a tremendous sheet of flame just abaft our bridge and we had been torpedoed [. . .] our cargo caught fire and there was a pretty big blaze. It was kerosene in that particular part of the ship. We all started to get the boats lowered, but the flames did not seem to get any bigger, so they

August 1942: Operation *Pedestal*

thought they would try to put it out. [Source: Commander D.E. Barton IWM 86/11/1]

Fortunately the fire was put out in about five minutes, thanks to Foamite extinguishers.

The hits on the *Cairo* and *Nigeria* were a very heavy blow indeed, as the two warships were the only vessels equipped with fighter direction equipment. This made the enemy's task much easier and the incidents of friendly fire increased. The naval liaison officer on the MV *Dorset* reported, for instance, that: 'on one occasion, after a heavy attack, three Spitfires flew over the ship [. . .] although several officers, including myself, ordered "cease fire" we had the great misfortune to shoot one down.' In mitigation he added that: 'it must be remembered that after the attacks we had been subjected to, the gunners were very excited and not in the mood to run risks . . .' The *Nigeria* had to turn back to Gibraltar, while the *Cairo* was so disabled – her stern had been blown off – that she had to be sunk.

The *Ohio* was ordered to detach itself from the convoy and take the inshore route. After a careful inspection of the damage done, the Master and Lieutenant Barton decided to keep to French territorial waters as long as possible and then sail independently to Malta, but they were then intercepted by HMS *Ledbury*, which ordered them to rejoin the convoy. By dawn on the 13th they were in sight of the convoy and had caught up by 9am.

In the meantime the convoy had suffered further serious casualties. At dusk an attack by a force of twenty German bombers and torpedo bombers fatally damaged both the *Empire Hope* and the *Clan Ferguson*, which according to Lieutenant Synes, the Naval Liaison officer on the *Dorset*, 'blew up after about four minutes [. . .] leaving a ghastly funeral pyre of burning petrol on the water.' Then the very same Ju 88 bomber that had hit *Clan Ferguson* torpedoed the *Dorset* in the bow. The forward bulkhead was flooded and the anchors and cables were rendered useless. As the ship was now a 'lame duck', which could only make a speed of 10 knots, it was decided she should leave the convoy and hug the Tunisian coast until Monastir, where she could then strike across to Malta during the night. 'Accordingly,' to quote Synes again, 'we turned south, and proceeded along close inshore, and were passed by all the remaining ships in the convoy

105

including to our surprise the *Ohio*. A destroyer attempted to round us up, so we advised him of our intentions and proceeded alone.'

That night and the following morning the convoy was to suffer yet further serious casualties. The merchant ships were dangerously strung out, and there was a reduced line of escorts, all of which offered rich picking for the E-Boats laying off Kelibia. The main bulk of the convoy passed Cape Bon at midnight, and forty minutes later the air attacks started. In a series of attacks lasting into the early morning HMS *Manchester* was the first ship to be torpedoed, and then the straggling merchantmen *Wairangi*, *Rochester Castle*, *Almeiria Lykes*, *Santa Eliza* and the *Glenorchy* were all hit. Only the *Rochester Castle* survived the attacks and was able to continue sailing with the main convoy.

Admiral Syfret, in his report on *Pedestal*, was highly critical of the decision to abandon the *Almeira Lykes*, which he regarded as a tale 'of shame'. When the decision was taken at 4.20am by the Captain, the Liaison Officer, Lieutenant Commander Mitchell, agreed with him, as the bows appeared to be going down rapidly and 'the crew would have most likely have gone anyway'. Mitchell was initially so distracted by having to teach the occupants of his lifeboat, who were British soldiers, to row that he was unable to get into contact with the other boats. These made a bee line for the escort vessel, which

---

Vichy France and Operation Pedestal

According to reports from the American Consul in Tunis, the seizure of three British officers by the Italians in the territorial waters of Vichy France caused 'a nasty incident'. The French insisted on their release and sent gendarmes to take them off the Italian boat. Captain Cossar's party reached the shore safely, and were found by two Italian peasants, who took them to their farm and gave them food, wine and cigarettes before they were handed over to Bonifichia Internment Camp. Altogether about 600 British prisoners were interned, and, to quote a report by one agent in Tunis, 'whilst passing through Tunis, they were greeted with shouts of *Vive les Anglais!*'

was probably the *Pathfinder*, only to be told to go back to the ship. In the meantime the *Almeiria*, although her bows were low in the sea, did not seem to be actually sinking. Nevertheless the crew refused point blank to go onboard again, and Marshall was left no option but to scuttle the ship. The crew was picked up by HMS *Eskimo* and *Somali* at 9.30am.

The crew of HMS *Manchester* was not so lucky. Before the ship was scuttled they had time to collect any personal items they wished, and then Captain Cossar ordered them to row towards the shore, where internment waited them. An Italian E-Boat appeared and seized three officers, but the majority of the *Manchester*'s crew made the shore, where they were interned by the Vichy French and were last seen being marched under guard to what appeared to Sergeant Major Mullens of the Royal Marines, who was rescued by a British cruiser, to be a 'castle'. They were interned until the Allied landing in North Africa in November 1942.

Dawn at least brought some relief from further attacks by MTBs, but the convoy was still in danger of being bombed from the air, and at one point it looked as if the Italian Fleet was going to intercept the group, as air reconnaissance had discovered a force of four cruisers and eight destroyers some 80 miles north of Western Sicily, steering south. Fortunately, under the impact of air attacks from Malta they turned east. At daybreak the *Rochester Castle*, *Waimarama* and *Melbourne Star* were in a single line with the cruisers *Kenya* and *Charybdis* in the front. *Ohio* was coming astern and joined the convoy at 7am. A handful of destroyers acted as a screen ahead of the convoy and others were rounding up stragglers, one of which was the *Dorset*, which came in form the north.

At about 8am three Savoias were sighted out of gunshot range to the south, flying very low. They made no attempt to attack but they distracted attention from a force of Ju 88s, which dived into the attack from another direction. The *Waimarama* received a direct hit, disintegrated, and burst into flames. Dennis Barton on the *Ohio* noted that: 'they were about a thousand feet high and covered about a quarter of a mile'. They were one of the 'grimmest things' he had seen in the war. The *Melbourne Star*, just two cables astern, was surrounded by flames, while debris cascaded over her. The gun crews in the rear of the ship thought she had been hit and jumped overboard to avoid the flames that were beginning to sweep the ship. As the Naval Liaison Officer reported:

> [The] Remainder of the men onboard tried to find the best means, if any, to escape but the ship came through the burning oil of the *Waimarama*, which was spreading rapidly and the men returned to the forecastle and so back to their action stations, the whole episode taking three minutes. The Second Officer who was in the wheel house with the helmsman at the time of the explosion rang on full speed [. . .] The speeding undoubtedly in my mind saved the ship. [Source: PRO ADM 199/1243]

When the *Melbourne* came out of the flames it was noticed that the cruiser, the *Ledbury*, was attempting to rescue the survivors from the inferno. Its captain, Lieutenant Commander Hill, had been so appalled by the way the Navy had abandoned merchant seamen in the Russian Convoy PQ-17 that he was determined to atone for what he regarded as a betrayal. Through his ship's efforts he managed to rescue forty men, twenty-three of whom had come from the *Melbourne Star*. One of these men later described how: '*Ledbury* kept right up to the flames going in and out at speed playing a hose right over the forecastle to keep the burning fuel from the survivors, and men from the ship's company of the *Ledbury* stripped and jumped overboard to help rescue them.'

Further attacks followed throughout the morning. The *Dorset* was hit and came to a halt, and the *Rochester Castle* was set on fire, but the flames were soon brought under control and she was able to continue sailing with the convoy. The *Dorset*'s crew abandoned ship at once and the master reported that her engine room was flooded, while a fire had also started in No. 4 Hold, which could not be put out. This was particularly dangerous as No. 5 Hold stored high octane fuel. At first the *Bramham* attempted to take her in tow, but when two Ju 88s appeared she rapidly abandoned the attempt, in order to give more effective AA cover. Later that afternoon, Captain Tuckett, her Master, the Naval Liaison Officer and two other officers

August 1942: Operation *Pedestal*

Convoy PQ-17

Convoy PQ-17 had sailed from Iceland to the USSR on 27 June 1942 with cargoes for the Soviet war effort. Fearing an attack from the *Tirpitz, Scheer, Lutzow* and *Hipper*, the convoy was told to scatter. German submarine and air forces were then able to sink nineteen of the unescorted merchantmen. However, it is arguable that if the convoy had not scattered the German warships would have been able to sink the whole of the convoy.

reboarded the *Dorset* to see if there was any realistic chance of the *Bramham* attempting a tow, but it soon became clear the fire on the ship was burning too strongly to be extinguished. She finally sank at 7pm after two further attacks by German bombers.

The *Ohio* was also in trouble. In one attack the guns of the *Ohio* shot down a Ju 88, the wing of which landed on her bridge. Then, as a result of several near misses, the electric fuel pumps were damaged and the ship's engines cut out. For a short time the steam fuel pump managed to maintain the *Ohio*'s speed at some 4 knots per hour, but this had to be reduced to 2½ and finally her engines packed up altogether again. The *Penn* attempted to take the *Ohio* in tow. Initially this seemed a feasible operation as her emergency steering gear was still working, but then her boilers broke down and she was left with no power at all and reduced to going around in circles. Attempts were made to work the rudder by hand but this was too slow to have any impact. The only hope was for the *Bramham* to steer the tow – i.e. act as the rudder – by being towed astern of the *Ohio*, but she was too busy with the *Dorset* to be spared.

At this stage it seemed that nothing could be done and that the ship was a sitting target. At 1.30pm her crewmen were transferred to the *Penn*, whose decks were already crowded with survivors from other torpedoed merchant ships. They were so dog tired that they sought out empty spaces on deck and dropped off to sleep immediately and could not be stirred when the *Penn*'s stewards brought round tea. At 4pm the Master, Captain Mason, managed to persuade the crew to return to the *Ohio*. Her rudder was disconnected and relieving tackles fitted, which made it possible to stop the ship from sheering too far to either side. She was again taken in tow by the *Penn*. The destroyer *Rye*, a minesweeper from Malta and two motor launches acted as stabilizers.

An hour later both the *Ohio* and the *Dorset* were attacked by four Ju 88s. The *Dorset* sank within twenty minutes, and the *Ohio* was hit in the engine room and appeared to be sinking. On the advice of the Master and the Chief Engineer, the crew once more abandoned ship. Yet despite further attacks, the *Ohio* stubbornly remained afloat, and after dark a working party returned onboard, secured the tows, so that the *Rye* towed ahead and the *Penn* made fast astern of the tanker in the hope that this would stop her swinging violently from side to side. Dennis Barton was pessimistic about the chances of the *Ohio* ever reaching the Grand Harbour. He wrote in his report later:

> I noticed that further damage to the ship had been done and that the deck was now buckled right across the ship where the mine had struck. She had obviously broken her back and was well down aft, having settled some 6 feet since leaving her at about 17.30 [5.30pm]. It seemed unlikely that she could remain afloat much longer.

However, initially during the night of 14/15 August some progress was made at 4 knots per hour, but at 1am the *Penn* rashly attempted to increase speed. This resulted in the Ohio swinging violently to port, snapping the tow line. Further attempts were made to steady her, but these too ended in failure. It was not until the following morning, when the *Penn* and *Bramham* were secured to her starboard and port sides respectively, that a relatively steady course could be set for Malta at 6½ knots.

Meanwhile the remaining three ships of the convoy were handed over at 4pm on the 13th to the minesweeping force from Malta, well within range of Spitfire cover from the island, and Admiral Burrough turned westward to sail back to Gibraltar with a force of two cruisers and five destroyers. Two hours later *Port Chalmers*, *Melbourne Star* and *Rochester Castle* entered the Grand Harbour.

August 1942: Operation *Pedestal*

The *Brisbane Star* also arrived safely at Malta. Since leaving the main convoy as a result of torpedo damage two days earlier, which had reduced her speed to 5 knots, she had hugged the North African coast and sailed through French territorial waters. Early in the morning of the 13th the *Brisbane Star*, which was flying no ensign, was spotted by an Italian Caproni torpedo bomber. The aircraft carried out a couple of dummy torpedo attacks and then flew off to the north. It reappeared when the *Brisbane Star* was just off Hammamet, circling and diving over her before flying off again. Captain Riley, the Master, remarked that: 'he [the pilot] was a gentleman, and observed the rules of war.' The fear was that a 'Teutonic gentleman' might arrive and deliver 'the coup de grâce', but fortunately that never came.

The French did not ignore the vessel. While sailing past Hammamet, Captain Riley fended off demands from the French authorities to anchor. The exchange of signals took place as follows:

Hammamet:	You should hoist your signal letters.
Brisbane Star:	Please excuse me.
Hammamet:	You should anchor.
Brisbane Star:	My anchors are fouled. I cannot anchor.
Hammamet:	You appear to be dragging your bow and stern anchors!
Brisbane Star:	I have no stern anchor.
Hammamet:	You should anchor *immediately*.
Brisbane Star:	I cannot anchor, my anchors are fouled.
Hammamet:	Do you require salvage or rescue?
Brisbane Star:	No.
Hammamet:	It is not safe to go too fast.

At the end of that exchange the *Brisbane Star* steamed away at a rate of 5 knots. Further along the coast she was stopped by a French launch, which fired a shot across her bows and boarded. They attempted to make the Captain take the ship into Susa harbour, but when he 'very diplomatically' refused and offered his guests a glass of whisky, 'they gave us their best wishes, noted down carefully our course and time of entry and leaving, and damage to the bows'. They also accepted one casualty who was not expected to live.

Campaign Chronicle

At dusk the *Brisbane Star* then set course at 11 knots for Malta. At 9.30pm the signals of an enemy submarine were picked up, reporting the movements of the ship and asking for aircraft by the Telegraphist, who 'had previously done much listening in to their waves and consequently could recognize the procedure'. At 6.30am on the 14th she was given Beaufighter protection from Malta, but an hour later was attacked by a Ju 88, which flew just 20 feet above the funnel, dropping heavy delayed action bombs each side of the ship. The *Brisbane Star* managed to arrive safely in the Grand Harbour at 3.30pm and was docked by 4.15pm.

By the evening of the 14th the *Ohio*, still with the *Penn* on one side and the *Bramham* on the other and protected by the *Ledbury* and units sent from Malta, was south-west of Filfla. The tug *Robust* and two mine sweepers, the *Beryl* and *Swona*, were sent out to meet her. There were no enemy air attacks at dusk, but the *Ohio* was far from safe. As the *Penn* and *Braham* manoeuvred the *Ohio* into the mine swept channel off Delimira Point, the towing wires gave way with a loud crack. The *Robust* then attempted to take the *Ohio* into tow but was not strong enough and collided with the *Penn*, holing her above water. The two cruisers were again secured to her and proceeded at snail's pace up the channel. On rounding Zonker Point the *Ohio* threatened to drift into the minefield, but eventually the arrival of more tugs stabilized her, and enabled her to be berthed at the Parlatorio Wharf at 9.45am on 15 August – Santa Marija Day.

On 13 August Alaric Rowntree, the Director of Communal Feeding, wrote in his diary that: 'all the island had been on tenterhooks for the last few days as everyone knew that a convoy was coming. The Italian radio said so . . .' Everywhere prayers were being said for its safe arrival, and its progress was followed with great anxiety on the island. The young RAF fitter and rigger, F.K. Rodgers, was voicing the feelings of the whole island when he wrote on the same day that: 'the only convoy news is sobering, its further toll of ships and men.' When the battered ships came in the atmosphere was 'electrifying' according to another serviceman and all the roads leading to the harbour were filled with hungry people. The cry 'Wasal il-konvoy! Diehel il-konvoy!' ('The convoy is here! The convoy is entering the harbour!') was raised. To catch a glimpse of it, people climbed on

August 1942: Operation *Pedestal*

rubble heaps and the bastions that surrounded the Grand Harbour. A band was playing and children were singing *Join the Navy and see the World* . . .

Unloading by both service personnel and Maltese workers started immediately, under Navy supervision, but transport from the dock-side to the storage depots was the work and responsibility of the Army. Some 250 army vehicles were provided plus the necessary technical backup. Special access roads, which would enable a rapid turn around had also been built to the depots. Altogether 3,000 men worked in three shifts day and night. By 23 August 12,000 tons of furnace oil, 3,600 tons of diesel oil and 32,000 tons of general cargo had all been unloaded. The Axis made no attempt to bomb any of the ships once they were well within range of the shore based fighters and had arrived in harbour. Yet, despite this impressive organization, some food was stolen and later appeared on the black market. A sailor onboard the *Melbourne Star*, for example, was offered £30 (approximately £800 in modern terms) for a sack of white flour by one of the Maltese workers.

From the ships that had been sunk there were 568 survivors. Some 207 of these sailed with the *Penn*, *Bramham* and *Ledbury* on the 18th and the remainder were flown out in due course. A fund was opened for the dependents of those who had died on the convoy and some £7,525 (approximately £230,000 in modern terms) was collected. The merchant sailors were very touched by the welcome given them, but taken aback by the lack of food and the quality of what existed. One sailor on the *Ohio*: 'felt quite sure that he had been given dog's meat to eat'. Inevitably there were also complaints about the delays in being flown back to Gibraltar. Another sailor remarked: 'we were received as heroes but they soon forgot about us.'

October 1942: The Luftwaffe's Last Offensive

Despite the arrival of the Pedestal *convoy, Malta is still under siege and dangerously short of food. Meanwhile, the RAF intensifies attacks on Axis convoys supplying Rommel in North Africa, and the Luftwaffe launches its final blitz.*

On 17 August Gort informed HQ Middle East that he 'would be grateful to receive your assurance that you will call upon Malta to engage only those targets which affect vitally the issue in the Western Desert, but must ask to continue to be consulted beforehand about any proposed strikes'. He was, as we have seen earlier, anxious to conserve aviation stocks. However, with the Eighth Army preparing for an offensive against Rommel, it was vital to weaken the Axis forces by preventing reinforcements reaching them from Italy. On 20 August the Air Officer, C-in-C Mediterranean sent a signal to Malta stressing that he attached 'supreme importance' to attacks on all southbound Axis convoys for the next ten days. Torpedo-carrying Beaufighters, escorted by Beauforts, scored considerable successes over the next two months. Each day usually brought news of the sinking of supply ships. The cracking of the German *Enigma* codes played a vital role in this success, as Rommel was informed of the sailing of every supply ship from Italy. Information on what each

October 1942: The Luftwaffe's Last Offensive

convoy contained and on the route it was taking was dispatched immediately to Air Vice Marshal Park. But to prevent the Germans becoming suspicious that their codes had been cracked, reconnaissance flights still continued.

On 21 August a 10,000-ton Italian tanker was sunk off Corfu, which meant the Italian forces in North Africa had to beg the Germans for a share of their increasingly scarce supplies of petrol. Rommel was desperate to renew his advance against Cairo, but was in urgent need of more ammunition and petrol. He told General von Rinteln, the German Military Attaché in Rome, that: 'Unless I get 2,000 cubic metres of fuel, 500 tons of ammunition by the 25th and a further 2,000 cubic metres of fuel by 27th and 2,000 tons of ammunition by 30th, I cannot proceed.' The Axis responded on 28 August by sending nine ships staggered over a period of six days. Again Beauforts operating from Malta managed to destroy five of these, including two tankers. On 1 September, as a result of lack of fuel, Rommel had to halt his advance.

Supply ships still continued to steam across the Mediterranean to Tripoli, but as Rommel was building up his forces to withstand the expected attack from Montgomery, every ship lost was an irreparable blow. Kesselring consequently decided to launch another air offensive against Malta. He calculated correctly that Malta was still short of food and fuel and that prolonged bombing would again neutralize her as an offensive base. He began reinforcing Sicily once more and managed to collect over 700 bombers and fighters. The blitz began at 7.20am on 11 October when seven Ju 88s, escorted by 25 Macchi 202s and four 109s approached Malta. This was followed by a further five raids and two night attacks. The blitz was relatively shortlived, lasting only two weeks, but its most intense period was the first three days. Thanks to Park's forward interception plan (see pages 98–9), the third Kesselring offensive was defeated: nevertheless, it took its toll of pilots and Spitfires. On 10 October, for instance, there were 113 Spitfires effective, but six days later this number had dwindled to fifty-six. The new GOC, Major General Scobie was particularly alarmed by this and personally drafted a telegram to Churchill demanding further supplies of pilots and Spitfires, which he gave to the Governor. Gort did not send off Scobie's telegram but he did cable the War Office his concerns about 'our dwindling Spitfire resources' and warned that: 'if we loose our present command of air over Malta, it may be difficult to retrieve . . .' However, by the end of the month it was clear the offensive had failed and the remnants of Fliegerkorps II were withdrawn to North Africa and Greece.

At the end of September Scobie, informed the Vice Chief of the Imperial General Staff, Lieutenant General Nye:

> Personally I have found everywhere the population most friendly, but considerable discontent exists, which may increase as the weather grows colder. The situation will, I am afraid be aggravated by the lack of proper accommodation and the glass to repair windows. I think discontent is most prevalent amongst the dockyard workers. The population is 70,000 and we should be gravely handicapped if it went sour on us. [Source: PRO WO 216/129]

On 13 September, in a ceremony deliberately designed to raise the spirits of the islanders, Lord Gort handed over the George Cross to Sir George Borg, who accepted the medal on behalf of the whole island. There is no doubt the gesture was appreciated, but unfortunately the award of the GC did nothing to solve the growing food problem.

The Santa Marija Convoy ensured some small improvement to the daily ration scale: the bread ration was increased for men between the ages of sixteen and sixty by 400 grams, a ration of kerosene was to be issued every week, instead of every fortnight, and from the beginning of September a ration of edible oil was also to be provided. On average the daily diet of the Maltese now consisted of 1,739 calories for workers and 1,496 for women and children. Increasingly the black market was becoming so expensive that the majority of the population could not afford to supplement their rations by buying on it.

Alaric Rowntree, the Director of the Communal Feeding Department was convinced that 'every available form of reserve will have been exhausted by the end of November' and gloomily foresaw

The Presentation of the George Cross, 13 September 1942

Lord Gort brought the George Cross with him from London when he replaced Dobbie as Governor. He handed the medal over to the Government of Malta very soon after he arrived, but had to wait until it was sufficiently safe to risk a public ceremony. By early September this seemed possible, as the air raids had died down. He chose Sunday 13 September, a date as near as possible to Malta Day (8 September), which commemorated the raising of the First Great Siege (see page 1). Sir George Borg, the Chief Justice of Malta, received it on behalf of Malta and her dependencies. The shortage of petrol ensured the crowd was limited to 4,000–5,000 people. Gort chose to hold the ceremony in the Palace Square, Valletta, partly because of its historical associations and partly because it was so well known to visitors and tourists in peace time. Also, on the wall of the Guard Room facing the Palace there was (and is still) an inscription in Latin recording the decision of the Treaty of Paris in 1814: 'To Great Britain, still unsubdued, these islands are entrusted by the Powers of Europe at the wish of the Maltese themselves . . .' In his report to the King, Gort aptly commented that: 'it has an appropriate ring about it today.' After the ceremony the medal went on a tour of the villages and towns of both Malta and Gozo.

the possibility of large-scale rioting if another convoy did not get through by November at the latest. He ominously confided in his diary that: 'if rioting does occur, it will not be like that of 1919, as there are now four or five thousand Maltese conscripted into the Army and an equal number of volunteers, who have arms and ammunition in their own homes.' According to Rowntree the farmers were 'already saying openly that sooner than sell at the equitably controlled prices they would prefer to be under Italian rule'. On 1 September the issue of deep frozen liver, the bitter taste of which the Maltese hated, triggered unrest at almost every Victory Kitchen, which now fed some 80,000 people a week. Rowntree reported that: 'an angry crowd of rioters stormed down to the food offices and could only be dispersed by promises that the liver would be replaced by corned beef.'

In an attempt to cut down on the number of mouths to feed, Gort pressed on with plans for evacuating the wives and children of British service personnel, as well as unemployed civilians and the chronically sick. The Colonial Office again opposed this policy on 30 October, as it felt the Maltese would draw the conclusion that 'the outlook for Malta [was] darkening' and that the Government 'are making haste to send their own kith and kin to safety, while there is yet time, but are content to leave the Maltese to their fate . . .' It argued that 'incalculable harm might be done to Anglo-Maltese relations which would take a generation to eradicate.' Gort, however, continued to press on with evacuation, but when a plane carrying women and children crashed in Gibraltar at the end of October, killing fifteen and injuring eleven, the War Cabinet intervened, curtailing evacuation on 3 November until further notice. However, the whole question of evacuation remained a sensitive topic. In December a proposal by the BBC to organize a Christmas party for children who had been evacuated from Malta – for propaganda purposes – was vetoed by the Ministry of Information on the grounds that:

Ideas for Beating the Blockade

By autumn 1942 a series of bizarre ideas for bringing in a trickle of supplies were being aired. 'Shrimp' Simpson, Captain of the Tenth Submarine Flotilla based at Malta suggested, for example, that submarines could tow cylinders packed with supplies, which would be disguised to look like pine trees. His ideas were abruptly rejected by the Admiralty. Another idea was put forward by a member of Gort's staff, who envisaged a 'food air lift' carried by Wellingtons, some of which could possibly tow gliders. However, none of these schemes was a realistic alternative to the dispatch of another convoy.

October 1942: The Luftwaffe's Last Offensive

a) our people of Malta will not be too pleased and b) that our friend Dr Goebbels could make quite a good story if he hasn't more important things to think about.

On 23 September Rowntree was sent to London to inform the Government of the food situation in Malta, and to press for the dispatch of another convoy – as big as possible – to be sent no later than November. When talking to officials and politicians in London, Rowntree found that they were not fully aware of 'how we are living hand to mouth and what a very little push is needed to send us over the edge to starvation and even collapse'. Indeed, the Chiefs of Staff seemed unconvinced when Rowntree met them on the 28th. The Air Chief Marshal, Sir Charles Portal, even suggested that: 'the Maltese should starve as the Russians are doing to feed their army.' But this was dismissed by the Chairman, Sir Alanbrooke, on the grounds that: 'the Maltese, unlike the Russians were not fighting for their very existence.' In the end the Chiefs of Staff agreed to a November convoy. Rowntree also managed to see Lord Woolton, the Minister of Food, who gave him a special message for Lord Gort to the effect that he was ready to do anything he could to help.

Gort and his officials were by no means sure the island would not have to face starvation. Rowntree, indeed, had to draw up contingency plans, which would have involved the slaughter of all livestock on the island, but the safe arrival on 20 November of Convoy MW-13, which consisted of four merchant vessels escorted by the 15th Cruiser Squadron, made such plans unnecessary. It was the first convoy to reach Malta without losses since August 1941. By the 26th their cargoes had been unloaded and dispersed to dumps throughout the island or else stored in deep rock shelters. Thankfully there were no raids by enemy aircraft. On the afternoon of 21 November Rowntree and a colleague went down to the harbour to see for themselves what was happening:

We went onboard the *Denbighshire* and watched them unloading flour, dried beans, corned beef, petrol, kerosene and bombs, including a number of huge 1,000-kilo ones, which were packed in among the flour (one slipped as it was being unloaded yesterday and fell right through the bottom of the lighter, sinking it). When one has known what the food situation has been for weeks and months, and has seen the starvation date inexorably drawing nearer and nearer, it is like the lifting of a tremendous burden to see the whole harbour a hive of industry with thousands of men, four thousand in all, busily employed getting the food safely stored before the enemy has a chance to sink the ships in harbour. Little tugs were chugging here and there with their trains of barges and each lighter point was piled up with unloaded cargo, which was being quickly transferred to waiting lorries which carried it to the safety of dumps and stores. We had an alert before leaving, but nothing developed and the 'raiders passed' went after a few minutes. [Source: IWM/A.W. Rowntree 02/8/1]

These four ships were sufficient to keep Malta going until the end of February. In December, however, a second convoy of nine merchant vessels arrived, M-14, with 58,500 tons of general cargo and two tankers with 18,220 tons of oil. As Simpson observed in his War Diary: 'the supply position, from being most precarious, became in this one month established on a firm basis.' The Siege of Malta had been broken.

The immediate consequence of this was a welcome increase in rations just before Christmas. Bread was increased from 14 oz to 21 oz per diem, the fat allowance was doubled and the daily cheese ration went up by ½ oz. Compared to the previous year, Christmas 1942 was a period of relative relaxation and calm. Gunner Fleming, for instance, enjoyed an enormous blow out of 'pork, plum pudding, mince pies, cheese, biscuits, etc.'

November 1942: The Siege is Raised

The intense bombing may have stopped, and the convoys are beginning to come in again, but the traumatic consequences of the siege have not vanished overnight. Although the Government has begun to think of reconstruction and post-war reform, expectations of immediate improvement are inevitably disappointed.

November 1942: The Siege is Raised

The raising of the Siege of Malta was gradual. Victory at Alamein in November 1942 made it possible for convoys to sail more safely from Egypt, but until Tunis fell six months later convoys from the west were still not safe. Even then Malta did not suddenly become an island of plenty. The shortage of shipping space, the demands for supplies by the Allied armies, as well as the impoverishment of the Mediterranean countries from which Malta used to import food, all inevitably delayed the recovery and replenishment of Malta. In the ruins of Valletta and the Three Cities thousands still lived in one-room shacks built from debris.

Understandably, however, the Maltese expected a marked improvement in their standard of living. Up to a point this did happen. Rations were increased and minor luxuries like tobacco came onto the market, but at a very high price. Meanwhile, the cost of repairs to damaged houses involved large – even excessive – sums being paid to builders and decorators. Consequently, wages that once seemed high – when there was little to spend them on – now seemed inadequate, and in August 1943 a strike broke out affecting all Service Departments and much of Civil Government too. It was eventually settled by the granting of increased subsidies and bonuses: but only after a second strike in the dockyard and some minor anti-British demonstrations in Valletta, where a crowd of some 300 indulged in 'some hissing and booing of English officers outside the Union Club'.

Increasingly, Gort was seen to be out of touch with the civil population. For example, in November 1943 the former Governor, General Sir Charles Bonham-Carter, heard from his Maltese contacts that Gort was: 'a very fine military leader, but he takes no interest in the Maltese and seems to dislike them. It was true that Gort – like his predecessor Dobbie – found Maltese politics and the Stricklands intensely irritating, and confided to Admiral Sir Dudley Pound on 9 September 1942 that: 'life here is an endless succession of what I term "tooth ache worries."' But both he and the British Government were aware of the need to modernize and rebuild Malta after all it had gone through. Gort fought hard to persuade the Cabinet to agree to the grant of £10 million as compensation for war damage in Malta. In December he also advised Cranborne that it was time to begin thinking about rebuilding Valletta and the Three Cities, and asked for expert advice from home. During the siege a succession of British experts had been flown in to Malta to advise on agriculture, water supplies, health and education. Their proposals were to form the basis of the reconstruction of Malta. As early as 11 August 1942 the Director of Education, A.V. Laferla, observed that the aim for post-war Malta should be to: 'develop the realm of the mind and make Malta a happier place to live in. We shall also, let us hope, abolish poverty from our midst and extirpate the slums in our cities.'

In August 1942 Joseph Sultana, the Maltese broadcaster in the BBC informed the Colonial Office that lack of self-government was the only grievance the Maltese felt 'irrespective of class or party', and the granting of this would have a far greater impact than the award of the George Cross. In December Gort confirmed this advice when he reported that the demand for self-government had 'emerged from the shelters with the temporary sounding of the all-clear' and had the backing of the Constitutional Party. Three months later he warned the Colonial Office that some announcement on the issue would have to be made, otherwise the local situation would worsen 'with an adverse impact on the secure working of the Government'. On 7 May 1943 he was permitted to inform the Maltese that they would be given self-government after the war.

Aftermath

The year 1943 witnessed the final triumph of Malta. On 9 May 1943 the Axis forces surrendered in Tunisia, and then on 8 September the news reached Malta that Italy had deserted the Axis and surrendered to the Allies. Three days later Malta enjoyed an exquisite moment of revenge, or, maybe irony is the more accurate word, when the Italian Fleet, in an attempt to escape capture and destruction at the hands of the Germans after the fall of Mussolini, steamed into the protection of the Grand Harbour. As one historian of Malta's war effort was to observe: 'the bulk of the large and strong Italian Fleet nestled within the waters of the small island it had once sought to subdue.' Consequently, Malta became an advance base for the invasion of Sicily, which took place on 10 July – just three years after the first Italian bombing raids.

The Siege of Malta was celebrated as one of the great epics of the war. King George VI, Churchill and Roosevelt all visited the island in the course of 1943. The Maltese were rightly celebrated for their courage and endurance in newspaper articles throughout the English-speaking world, yet there was an undercurrent of criticism and possibly jealousy of the praise heaped upon them. Lord Gort feared this publicity would create 'an atmosphere of self-satisfaction'. Peter Lunn, a lieutenant in the RA, who submitted to the Colonial Office a proposal to write a history of the siege at the end of 1942, observed that:

> the Maltese have so exaggerated their own courage and endurance in this war, that there are only too many people itching to debunk them as soon as publishers are freed from the cloying hand of censorship. As a result the air will be thick with flying bouquets and brickbats and the true story [. . .] [of] one of the world's classics will be obscured. [Source: PRO CO 23/1839]

The Siege of Malta

Looking back over sixty years from the end of the Second World, is it possible to adopt a revisionist line on the Siege of Malta? The siege was not as long as Leningrad, where starvation was a reality, nor was Malta both fought over and bombed, as was Stalingrad. The ruthless carpet bombing that Germany was subjected to was also on a far greater scale than anything Malta had to endure. Yet the historian must not fall into the trap of playing down the Siege of Malta. It was the first air siege in history, and the aerial bombardment of Valletta and the Three Cities, especially from January to May 1942 was more intense than anything Britain had to withstand. A. V. Laferla, the Director of Education in Malta, called it a 'holocaust'.

But it was a siege that waxed and waned. Until the *'Illustrious* blitz' in January 1941 Malta did receive regular supplies by convoy and the bombing was light. This changed abruptly with the first Kesselring offensive. And yet, when the German planes were withdrawn to Crete and the Russian Front in May/June 1941, Malta enjoyed some six months remission from the bombing: only for the noose to tighten with a vengeance when the Germans decided to neutralize Malta in a series of intense air attacks lasting from January to May 1942. Even when these attacks eased, Axis domination of the Mediterranean, combined with Rommel's advance into Egypt, ensured that sailing a convoy through to Malta was a dangerous and costly operation. The few merchant ships that managed to make it to the Grand Harbour in the convoys of June and August 1942 brought insufficient supplies, and even though the air battle was decisively won in October, the hunger worsened and morale sank to its lowest point in the whole siege. It was only with the defeat of Rommel's Afrikakorps at El Alamein and the subsequent occupation of the ports in Cyrenaica, that the crucial convoys in November and December reached Malta without loss.

One thread running through the official correspondence is the fear that the morale of the Maltese would crack. Yet, although the last three months of hunger (from August to September 1942) brought an increasing desperation, the demands for peace never became widespread, and loyalty to Britain remained constant. In a post-imperial age this is arguably difficult to understand. One reason, certainly, was that the Naval Dockyard and the services were by far the largest employers in Malta, and there was no guarantee that Italian rule

Aftermath

could offer any better material prospects. The British Government was also backed by the Constitutional Party, which had done much to neutralize Italian influence in the island during the 1930s – even though it was often critical of British policy in Malta. Governors Bonham-Carter, Dobbie and Gort were all intensely aware of Maltese public opinion and constantly pressed the British Government to grant subsidies and pensions and make generous grants available for reconstruction. The Colonial Office took care to ensure that Malta was not ignored in her ordeal by the BBC and British press, and Mountbatten's idea of the award of the George Cross to the whole island was an inspired piece of public relations. The Maltese were also an intensely religious people, who had the spiritual strength to withstand the hardships of the bombing and the lack of food. Of crucial importance, too, were the tunnels and shelters carved deep into the rock, which provided effective protection against the bombs.

As in all military campaigns, the second Siege of Malta was broken through a mixture of factors. Certainly the skills of the gunners, bravery of the fighter pilots and the supply of Spitfires from March 1942 onwards played a key role, as did the bitter struggle to push through supplies to the island at a time when the Royal Navy had lost control of the Mediterranean. However, the mistakes of the Axis powers also gave Malta a vital break, just at the point when defeat seemed inevitable. In June 1940 Mussolini could probably have seized Malta, and in May 1941 and May 1942 the opportune transfer of Fliegerkorps X and II to Russia and Crete almost certainly saved it.

The Siege of Malta was an heroic epic by any standards, but to what extent was it worth it? The historian Corelli Barnett calls it a 'Mediterranean Verdun', which sucked British forces into a debilitating battle of attrition. Before the war, Air Force and Army representatives on the Committee of Imperial Defence warned that it would be impossible to keep the Grand Harbour and naval dockyards open if air superiority was lost over Malta, and as events were to show, this proved correct. As early as 1940 Malta ceased to be a viable base for the Mediterranean Fleet, and in the spring of 1942 even the submarine flotilla had to be withdrawn. At that stage it can be argued that Malta had become a liability and that *Harpoon*, *Vigorous* and *Pedestal* squandered men and materiel on an island that had become a drain on resources. Corelli Barnett argues that

The Siege of Malta

after the ignominious fall, first of Singapore in February 1942, and then Tobruk in June, the decision to hold Malta at all costs was taken for political rather than strategic reasons, and that a strictly rational policy would have dictated its surrender. He goes on to draw his readers' attention to recent research, which shows that between July and October 1942 Rommel 'actually received larger quantities of fuel than in February–June when he was preparing for his summer offensive'.

Yet war cannot be fought without the political dimension, and the fall of Malta at that stage would surely have delivered an incalculable blow to British prestige at a stage when Rommel was advancing rapidly in Africa. While Malta could not serve as a safe base for the Mediterranean Fleet, it was an invaluable base for striking at the convoys supplying the Axis forces in North Africa. In June–December 1941, and then from June 1942 onwards, considerable damage was done to the Axis supply lines by bombers and submarines based in Malta. They effectively prevented Rommel from using Tobruk as a forward harbour for his advance. Malta was also an important base for reconnaissance of enemy naval movements in the Mediterranean. The fact that Kesselring came to the conclusion that the neutralization of Malta 'was the indispensable precondition [. . .] for establishing secure lines of communication between Italy and North Africa' confirms its strategic value. It was indeed worth fighting to defend.

Appendix I:
The Siege of Malta in Seven Acts

I   June–December 1940:
        the first Italian offensive.

II   January–May 1941:
        the first German offensive, heralded by the '*Illustrious* blitz'.

III   June–December 1941:
        the Allied offensive from Malta on Axis supply lines to North Africa, following the redeployment of Fliegerkorps X from Sicily to North Africa and Russia.

IV   January–May 1942:
        the second German offensive, executed by Luftflotte II.

V   June–August 1942:
        the establishment of local air superiority over Malta. But following Axis advances in North Africa the island was still besieged, and both the *Harpoon* and *Pedestal* convoys suffered enormous losses.

VI   October 1942:
        the final Luftwaffe offensive – an unsuccessful attempt to neutralize the RAF.

VII November–December 1942:
        the breaking of the siege with the arrival of convoys *Stoneage* and *Portcullis*.

Appendix II:
Naval Strength in the Mediterranean 1940

	Royal Navy		Italian Navy
	Alexandria	*Gibraltar*	
Ships			
Battleships	4	1	6
Carriers	1	1	0
8-inch Cruisers	0	0	0
6-inch Cruisers	8	1	12
Destroyers	20	9	57
Torpedo Boats	0	0	71
Submarines	12	0	115

This Table is adapted from David Thomas, *Malta Convoys*, Leo Cooper, 1999.

Notes

a) Four Italian battleships dated from the First World War; two, the *Vittoria Veneto* and the *Littorio*, were completed in August 1940.

b) In the Admiralty files in the National Archives (PRO ADM 119/2008) the following extract from an article in the Italian paper, *La Stampa*, is translated and filed. It was written on 15 August 1942 during the climax of the Axis operations to stop the *Pedestal* convoy reaching Malta:

> while the carrier is a rich country's weapon, the U-Boat is the classic weapon of a poor country. The former is made

Appendix II

and moved by one factor: gold. The U-Boat depends above all on those who inhabit it, on their faith, their courage, their intelligence and spirit of sacrifice; its greatest factor is the real blood, pure and strong, of the men on board.

Appendix III:
The Malta Convoys

Fleet Code	Convoy	From	Sailed*	Sunk	Turned Back	Arrived	Date
MB-3	MF-2	East	3			3	01.09.40
MB-6	MF-3	East	4			4	11.10.40
MB-8	MW-3	East	5			5	09.11.40
MB-9	MW-4	East	4			4	26.11.40
Collar		West	2			2	29.11.40
MC-2	MW-5	East	8			8	20.12.40
MC-4	MW-5½	East	2			2	10.01.41
Excess		West	1			1	10.01.41
MC-9	MW-6	East	4			4	23.03.41
MD-3		East	1			1	21.04.41
MD-4	MW-7	East	7			7	09.05.41
Substance	GM-1	West	7		1	6	24.07.41
Halberd	GM-2	West	9			8	28.09.41
MF-1		East	1			1	18.12.41
MF-2		East	1			1	08.01.42
MF-3	MW-8	East	4	1		3	19.01.42
MF-4		East	1			1	27.01.42
MF-5	MW-9	East	3	2	1	0	
MG-1	MW-10	East	4	1		3	23.03.42
Harpoon	GM-4	West	6	4		2	16.06.42
Vigorous	MW-11	East	11	2	9	0	
Pedestal	GM-5	West	14	9		5	15.08.42
Stoneage	MW-13	East	4			4	20.11.42
Portcullis	MW-14	East	5			5	05.12.42

* number of merchant ships sailed

Appendix III

There were also seven attempts by unescorted merchantmen to reach Malta. Of these only one was successful; three were sunk; two captured and one turned back.

Table adapted from: David Thomas, *Malta Convoys*, Leo Cooper, 1999, p. 197.

Appendix IV:
The Composition of the Key Convoys, Their Naval Escorts and the Axis Forces Operating Against Them, July 1941–August 1942

A) Operation *Substance* (July 1941)
ALLIED VESSELS

MERCHANTMEN
Melbourne Star, *City of Pretoria*, *Sydney Star*, *Durham*, *Deucalion*, *Port Chalmers*, *Leinster*

The *Leinster* ran aground in the Straits of Gibraltar and did not sail with the convoy.

CLOSE ESCORT (FORCE H)
Renown (battle cruiser)
Ark Royal (aircraft carrier)
Hermione (anti-aircraft cruiser)
Faulknor, *Fearless*, *Foxhound*, *Firedrake*, *Foresight*, *Fury*, *Forester* and *Duncan* (destroyers)
This force was strengthened by units from the Home Fleet: *Nelson* (battleship)
Edinburgh (flagship of Rear Admiral Syfret), *Manchester*, *Arethusa* (cruisers),
Cossack, *Maori*, *Sikh*, *Nestor* (Royal Australian Navy), *Lightening*, *Farndale*, *Avondale* and *Eridge* (destroyers)

Appendix IV

B) Operation *Halberd* (August 1941)
ALLIED VESSELS

MERCHANTMEN
Breconshire, Imperial Star, City of Calcutta, Ajax, Dunedin Star, Clan Ferguson, Rowallan Castle, Clan Macdonald, City of Lincoln

CLOSE ESCORT
Prince of Wales, Nelson and *Rodney* (battleships)
Kenya, Edinburgh, Sheffield and *Euryalus* (cruisers)
Duncan, Legion, Lance, Lively, Ghurkha, Oribi, Fury, Farndale, Heythorp, Piorun (Polish), *Garland* (Polish), *Isaac Sweers* (Dutch) (destroyers)

COVERING FORCE (FORCE H)
Ark Royal (aircraft carrier)
Hermione (anti-aircraft cruiser)
Cossack, *Zulu, Foresight, Forester, Laforey, Lightening* (destroyers)
Brown Ranger (tanker) and *Fleur de Lys* (corvette – for refuelling the destroyers)
Utmost, Trusty and *Sokol* (Polish) (submarines)

AXIS FORCES (ITALIAN)
Littorio, Vittorio Veneto (battleships)
Trento, Trieste, Gorzia (heavy cruisers)
Duca Degli, Abruzzi (light cruisers)
11 Submarines
    Adapted from: David Thomas, *Malta Convoys*, Leo Cooper, 1999, p. 197.

The Siege of Malta

C) Operation *Harpoon* (From Gibraltar, June 1942)
ALLIED VESSELS

MERCHANTMEN
Troilus, Burdwan, Chant, Tanimbar, Orari, Kentucky

CLOSE ESCORT
Cairo, Bedouin, Marne, Matchless, Ithuriel, Partridge, Blankney, Middleton, Badsworth, Kujawiak (Polish) (cruisers)
ML *Welshman*
Hebe, Speedy, Rye, Hythe (mine sweepers)
6 MTBs

COVERING FORCE
Malaya (battleship)
Argus (aircraft carrier) with 4 Fulmars and 4 Swordfish, Eagle with 9 Swordfish & 4 Sea Hurricanes
Kenya, Charybdis, Liverpool, Onslow (cruisers)
Icarus, Escapade, Wishart, Westcott, Wrestler, Vidette, Antelope (destroyers)
T Brown Ranger, Coltsfoot (Tanker Force – Force Y)

Appendix IV

D) Operation *Vigorous* (From Alexandria, June 1942)
ALLIED VESSELS

MERCHANTMEN
Pretoria, City of Calcutta, FR Bhutan, FR Potaro, Bulkoil, Rembrandt, Aagtekerk, City of Edinburgh, City of Lincoln, Elizabeth Bakke, Ajax

CLOSE ESCORT
Delphinium, Primula, Erica, Snapdragon (corvettes)
Boston, Seham (mine sweepers)
Griffin, Hotspur, Fortune, Dulverton, Exmoor, Croome, Eridge, Airedale, Beaufort, Hurworth, Tetcott, Aldenham (destroyers)

COVERING FORCE
Cleopatra, Dido, Hermione, Euryalus, Arethusa, Coventry, Birmingham, Newcastle (cruisers)
Napier, Nestor, Nizam, Norman, Ran (7th Destroyer Flotilla)
Parkenham, Paladin, Inconstant (12th Destroyer Flotilla)
Jervis, Kelvin, Javelin (14th Destroyer Flotilla)
Sikh, Zulu, Hasty (22nd Destroyer Flotilla)
Centurion (an old wireless controlled target ship mocked up to look like a modern battleship)
Antwerp, Malines (rescue ships)

BRITISH SUBMARINES
Proteus, off Taranto
Thorn, off Taranto
Taku, off Taranto
Thrasher, off Taranto
Porpoise, off Taranto
Una, off Taranto
P31, off Taranto
P34, off Taranto
P35, off Taranto
P211, between Sicily & Sardinia
P42, between Sicily & Sardinia
P43, between Sicily & Sardinia
P46, between Sicily & Sardinia

The Siege of Malta

AXIS FORCES (ITALIAN)

SURFACE FORCES DEPLOYED AGAINST OPERATION *HARPOON*
Eugenio di Savoia, Montecuccoli (cruisers)
Oriani, Ascari, Zeno, Gioberti, Vivaldi, Malocello, Premuda (destroyers)

SURFACE FORCES DEPLOYED AGAINST OPERATION *VIGOROUS*
Littorio, Vittorio Veneto (battleships)
Trieste, Gorizia (heavy cruisers)
Garibaldi, Duca d'Aosta (light cruisers)
Twelve destroyers of the 7th, 13th and 11th Flotillas

ITALIAN SUBMARINES
Malachite, stationed N. of Algerian Coast
Velella, stationed N. of Algerian Coast
Bronzo, stationed N. of Algerian Coast
Emo, stationed N. of Algerian Coast
Uarsciek, stationed N. of Algerian Coast
Giada, stationed N. of Algerian Coast
Acciaio, stationed N. of Algerian Coast
Otaria, stationed N. of Algerian Coast
Alagi, stationed N. of Algerian Coast
Corallo, deployed near Malta
Dessie, deployed near Malta
Onice, deployed near Malta
Ascianghi, deployed near Malta
Aradam, deployed near Malta
Axum, deployed in Ionian Sea
Platino, deployed in Ionian Sea
Micca, deployed in Ionian Sea
Zoea, deployed in Ionian Sea
Atropo, deployed in Ionian Sea
Galatea, deployed further east of Ionian Sea group
Sirena, deployed further east of Ionian Sea group

Appendix IV

U-BOATS
U-77, U-81, U-205, U-431, U-453, U-559

MTB GROUP DEPLOYED AGAINST OPERATION *VIGOROUS*
6 MTBs of the 3rd MTB Flotilla

The Siege of Malta

E) Operation *Pedestal* or the Santa Marija Convoy (August 1942)

MERCHANTMEN
Almeira Lykes, Brisbane Star, Clan Ferguson, Deucalion, Dorset, Empire Hope, Glenorchy, Melbourne Star, Ohio, Port Chalmers, Rochester Castle, Santa Elisa, Waimarama, Wairangi

CLOSE ESCORT (FORCE Z)
Nelson and *Rodney* (battleships)
Victorious (16 Fulmars), *Indomitable* (10 Martlets, 24 Sea Hurricanes, 16 Albacores), *Eagle* (16 Sea Hurricanes), *Furious* (42 Spitfires to be flown off to Malta, 4 Albacores), *Argus* (6 Sea Hurricanes) (aircraft carriers)
Phoebe, Sirius, Charybdis (light cruisers)
Laforey, Lightening, Lookout, Quentin, Somali, Eskimo, Tartar, Ithuriel, Antelope, Wishart, Vansittart, Westcott, Zetland, Wilton (destroyers)

COVERING FORCE (FORCE X)
Nigeria, Kenya, Manchester, Cairo (light cruisers)
Ashanti, Intrepid, Icarus, Foresight, Fury, Pathfinder, Penn, Derwent, Bramham, Bicester, Ledbury, Badsworth (destroyers)
Brown Ranger, Dingledale (Fleet oilers)
Jonquil, Geranium, Spirea, Coltsfoot (corvettes)
Jaunty, Salvonia (tugs)

MALTA ESCORT FORCE
Speedy, Rye, Hebe, Hythe (17th Minesweeping Flotilla)
3rd Motor Launch Flotilla (7 launches)
Safari, Unbroken, Uproar, Ultimatum, Unruffled, Utmost, United, Una, P.222 (submarines)

Appendix IV

AXIS FORCES (ITALIAN)

Gorizia, Bolzano, Trieste (heavy cruisers)

Aviera, Gerniere, Camiciai Nera, Legionario, Ascari, Corsaro, Grecale (destroyers)

Eugenio di Savoia, Muzio Attendolo, Raimondo Montecuccoli (light cruisers)

Maestrale, Gioberti, Oriani, Fuciliere (destroyers)

Malocello (mine laying destroyer)

Velella, Bronzo, Emo, Giada, Otaria, Alagi, Dessie, Otaria, Ascianghi, Asteria, Avorio, Axum, Bronzo, Brin, Cobalto, Dandolo, Dagubur, Granito, Otaria, Uarsciek, Wolframio (submarines)

19 MTBs

AXIS FORCES (GERMAN)

U-7, U-205, U-333

4 MTBs

Adapted from Peter Smith, *Pedestal: The Malta Convoy of August 1942*, William Kimber, London 1970

Appendix V: Malta's Air Defences

The Airfields

LUQA

Before 1938 the airfield at Luqa was merely a grass landing strip. Later, four paved runways were constructed, and on 1 April 1940 it became an RAF station. Its first operational unit, which became effective on 1 September, was No. 439 Squadron (reconnaissance). At the end of 1940 Luqa suffered frequent and severe air raids, but the respite from bombing, May–December 1941, allowed the extension of the North West–South East runway. Luqa was heavily bombed again, January–May 1942.

FLYING UNITS AT LUQA 1940–42

Unit	Aircraft Type	Date in	Date out
431	Maryland, Blenheim, Skua	Sept. 40	Jan. 41
Malta Well. Flt	Wellington	Oct. 40	Dec. 40
37 Sqd., Det.	Wellington	Nov. 40	Dec. 40
148 Sqd.	Wellington	Dec. 40	Mar. 41
69 Sqd.	Wellington, Beaufort, Hurricane	(Ex-431)	Oct. 41
78 Sqd.	Whitley V	Feb. 41	Feb. 41
139 Sqd., Det.	Blenheim IV	May 41	Jun. 41
252 Sqd., Det.	Beaufighter I	May 41	May 41
110 Sqd., Det.	Blenheim IV	Jul. 41	Aug. 41
105 Sqd., Det.	Blenheim IV	Jul. 41	Sept. 41
38 Sqd., Det.	Wellingon Ic	Aug. 41	Oct. 41
107 Sqd., Det.	Blenheim IV	Aug. 41	Jan. 42
113 Sqd., Det.	Blenheim	Sept. 41	Sept. 41

Appendix V

Unit	Aircraft Type	Date in	Date out
104 Sqd., Det.	Wellington II	Oct. 41	Jan. 42
18 Sqd., Det.	Blenheim IV	Oct. 41	Jan. 42
40 Sqd.	Wellington Ic	Oct. 41	May 42
69 Sqd.	Maryland I, Spitfire, Beaufort, Wellington Ic	Nov. 41	Feb. 44
21 Sqd.	Blenheim IV	Dec. 41	Mar. 42
2 Pru Det.	Beaufighter	Dec. 41	Apr. 42
221 Sqd., Det.	Wellington VIII	Jan. 42	Aug. 42
126 Sqd.	Spitfire Vc	May 42	Jun. 43
217 Sqd., Det.	Beaufort II	Jun. 42	Aug. 42
39 Sqd., Det.	Beaufort I	Jun. 42	Aug. 42
1435 Flt/Sqd.	Spitfire Vb, Vc	Jul. 42	Jun. 43
227 Sqd.	Beaufighter VI	Aug. 42	Nov. 42
39 Sqd. (reformed)	Beaufort I	Aug. 42	Dec. 42
113 Sqd., Det.	Wellington	Sept. 42	Sept. 43
104 Sqd., Det.	Wellington II	Nov. 42	Jan. 43
40 Sqd.	Wellington III	Nov. 42	Jan. 43
148 Sqd.	Wellington Ic	Dec. 42	Dec. 42
23 Sqd.	Mosquito II, VI	Jan. 43	Dec. 43

Det. = Detachment

HAL FAR

This airfield was opened by the Governor on 16 January 1923 and initially used by the Fleet Air Arm. On 18 April 1941 it was put on alert, being heavily bombed in March 1941 and from February–April 1942.

The Siege of Malta

FLYING UNITS AT HAL FAR 1940–42

Unit	Aircraft Type	Date in	Date out
Fighter flight	Gladiator	Apr. 40	Apr. 40
Fighter flight	Gladiator, Hurricane	May 40	Aug. 40
767 Sqd.	Swordfish I	Jun. 40	Jul. 40
830 Sqd. (ex 767)	Swordfish I	Jul. 40	Mar. 42
261 Sqd.	Gladiator, Hurricane	Aug. 40	Nov. 40
418 Flt	Hurricane I	Aug. 40	Aug. 40
185 Sqd.	Hurricane I, IIa, IIb	May 41	Jun. 43
800X Flt	Fulmar	May 41	Nov. 41
828 Sqd.	Albacore I	Oct. 41	Mar. 42
605 Sqd.	Hurricane	Jan. 42	Jan. 42
229 Sqd.	Hurricane	Mar. 42	Apr. 42
RNA Sqd.	Albacore, Swordfish	Mar. 42	Dec. 42
821 Sqd.	Albacore	Nov. 42	Jun. 43
828 Sqd.	Albacore	Dec. 42	Jun. 43

TA' QALI

Before the war Ta' Qali had served as Malta's civilian airport, and was used by the Italian airlines until they moved to Luqa in April 1940. The first RAF squadron landed there in October 1940, and it officially became 'RAF Ta' Qali' on 20 November. In April 1941 work started on excavating underground operation rooms and building dispersal tracks. A 12,000-gallon fuel tank was also constructed underground. In the heavy raids from January–April 1942 most of the buildings above ground were destroyed. See table on facing page.

Appendix V

Unit	Aircraft Type	Date in	Date out
261 Sqd.	Hurricane I	Nov. 40	May 41
249 Sqd.	Hurricane I, Ia, Ib	May 41	Nov. 42
238 Sqd.	Hurricane I	Jun. 41	Jun. 41
Malta NFU	Hurricane	Jul. 41	Dec. 41
69 Sqd.	Hurricane IIa, Maryland I	Oct. 41	Nov. 43
1435 Flt	Hurricane, Beaufighter	Dec. 41	Jul. 42
605 Sqd.	Hurricane IIb	Feb. 42	Feb. 42
603 Sqd.	Spitfire Vc	Apr. 42	Aug. 42
229 Sqd.	Spitfire Vc	Aug. 42	Dec. 42
272 Sqd.	Beaufighter I, VI	Nov. 42	Jun. 43

SAFI DISPERSAL TRACK

This was completed as an airfield in February 1943. In 1941–42 it was used as a dispersal track for aircraft where they were protected by pens from bombing raids.

QUERENDI

Work began on building an airfield at Querendi in October 1940. During the two 'Kesselring blitzes' of 1941 and 1942 Querendi acted as a decoy. It opened as a fully functional airfield in November 1942.

KALAFRANA

This base was first opened in 1915 for Royal Naval sea planes. By September 1940 the Sunderland Flying Boats of No. 228 Squadron were based there, but in March 1941 they moved to Aboukir. Kalafrana then became a staging post for flying boats passing through the Mediterranean. For a time some Free French reconnaissance units were based there. One sea plane, He 115A-2, which belonged to the Royal Norwegian Navy, had German markings and was used to pick up British agents in Tripoli.

These statistics are adapted from John F. Hamlin, *Military Aviation in Malta 1915–1993*, GMS Enterprises, Peterborough 1994.

Appendix VI: Malta's Land Defences

In 1939 the Chiefs of Staff had agreed that Malta needed 112 heavy, 60 light anti-aircraft guns with 24 searchlights and seven battalions of infantry in addition to the Kings Own Malta Regiment (KOMR). When war broke out in September 1939 the Malta garrison consisted of the following battalions:

2nd Devons
1/1 Dorsets
2nd Royal Irish Fusiliers
2nd Royal West Kents
1 Kings Own Malta Regiment
(The KOMR had been disbanded in 1921, but reconstituted ten years later)

In August 1939 this force was given brigade status, and the battalions were allotted the following operational areas:

i   The KOMR, the north
ii   The Royal Irish Fusiliers, the south coast
iii The Queen's Own Royal West Kents, Marsaxlokk Bay
iv   The Dorsets, coast to the east of Valletta
v   The Devons, held in reserve at Attard in the middle of the island

On 21 September the KOMR raised a second battalion and the forces stationed on Malta were upgraded to a division. When the first Kesselring bombing offensive began in January 1941, Malta had six of the seven required battalions, and the following Month troops

Appendix VI

from the Cheshire and Hampshire Regiments arrived. By August 1941 the garrison was increased to a combatant strength of 22,000 and consisted of:

Battalions and Their Length of Time Stationed in Malta

i	Four battalions of the Kings Own Malta Regt (continuous)
ii	2 Bn The Royal Irish Fusiliers 1939–43
iii	2 Bn The Queen's Own Royal West Kents 1939–43
iv	8 Bn King's Own Royal Border Regt 1940–44
v	4 Bn The Royal East Kent Regt (the Buffs) 1940–43
vi	1 Bn Hampshire Regt 1941–43
vii	8 Bn Manchesters 1940–43
viii	1 Bn Durham Light Infantry 1941–43
ix	2 Bn Devonshire Regt 1938–43
x	1 Bn the Cheshire Regt 1941–43
xi	11 Bn The Lancashire Regt 1941–44

Besides its anti-invasion role, the main duties of the garrison were: patrols, clearing of streets blocked by rubble, keeping air bases operational, constructing aircraft pens and providing personnel for manhandling planes.

By August 1941 after the arrival of Convoys *Substance* and *Style* the anti-aircraft armament in Malta consisted of 112 heavy and 118 light guns. The AA units on Malta consisted of:

a) 7th Light Anti-Aircraft Brigade
   32nd 65th, 74th Light AA Regts, 3rd Light AA Regt RMA, 4th Searchlight RA/RMA
b) 10th Heavy Anti-Aircraft Brigade
   4th, 7th, 10th Heavy AA Regt RA, 2nd, 11th Heavy AA Regts RMA
c) Unbrigaded Units
   225th Light AA Battery RA; 14th heavy AA (Relief) Battery RMA

Appendix VII:
An Interview with Godwin Castaldi by the Author on 12 September 2006

———⟫•✧•⟪———

Godwin was born in Vittoriosa in 1930. His father worked in the naval dockyards. In 1937 the family moved a few miles away to Paolo. In June 1940, after three houses in the town had been bombed by the Italians, the family moved out to Birkirkara, where they managed to rent a house. Within a couple of months, however, they returned to Paolo, as they did not want their large and comfortable house, which had two bathrooms, to be requisitioned for military use. At this stage the Italian raids no longer seemed terrifying, and with his friends he would often go up on the hill to watch the dogfights. They were particularly dismissive of the Italians, who 'would fly as high as possible and drop their bombs in the sea. Nobody cared about them.'

Even if the Italians themselves apparently represented no major threat, his life was dominated by the war. His school was taken over by the Army and, like so many of his contemporaries, he was taught in a church: in his case Santa Marija at Toxien, a few miles from Paolo. He had two cousins who had volunteered to serve in the Dockyard Defence Battery. He would often climb up to their positions and chat to the soldiers. When the RMA had a party, their English captain would borrow glasses from his parents.

With the beginning of the *'Illustrious* blitz' in January 1941, like so many others on the island, he learnt 'what war was like'. By this time deep shelters had been dug through the rock in every other street in

Appendix VII

Paola. These consisted of two long tunnels connected with three exits, one on each end and one in the centre. Godwin's family was able to afford to pay labourers to dig out a private room, about 8ft by 6ft, where his father built bunk beds. On the second day of the 'Illustrious blitz' he remembers coming back from school just as an air raid was starting. He was met by his mother, and they hurried home through devastated streets. As soon as they reached their house another raid occurred and they went straight down into the shelter.

For the first four months of both 1941 and 1942 it became routine to spend the nights and much of the day in the shelters. The noise of the bombs landing and guns firing was deafening. Godwin and his friends used to laugh at the old ladies telling their rosaries and begging the Virgin Mary 'to throw the bombs on the fields'. He continued to go to school, but frequently lessons in Santa Marija were interrupted by raids and the children and their teachers went down into a shelter where lessons continued. He remembers clearly sitting on a long bench down there with his class, while the teacher stood in front talking to them.

I asked Godwin whether, as a child, he found the bombing traumatic. He obviously did see some horrific sights. One image he clearly recalls was when, after church on a Sunday, an aerial torpedo hit the middle of the street and made a large hole. He remembers 'bits of horses flying everywhere'. He was upset 'for just a day', and soon recovered. Although his neighbours' two sons (who served in the Dockyard Defence Battery), many of his father's colleagues in the dockyard, and individual soldiers whom he got to know – such as Morris in the Dorsets, who drove the Scammel – were killed, he was fortunate that his immediate family survived, and consequently this gave him a certain feeling of security.

On Maundy Thursday 1942, when he and his friends were returning home, the air raid siren went. Initially they sat on the parapet steps to see what was happening, but then, when they saw fifteen German planes coming in sets of five, they ran for the middle door of the shelter. As they got down inside they heard an enormous roar and the shelter seemed to shake. Godwin's father raced up, followed by his son, and saw that their house and three others were just a pile of rubble.

The Siege of Malta

His mother was crying because she had hidden silver, money and other precious items under the stairs for safe keeping. His cousin, a surgeon, dug around in the dust with his bare hands and managed to find one of the baskets, which contained silver spoons that he treasures to this day.

By 1942 war was the regular backdrop to his life. The raids could be terrifying but they were also good theatre for adventurous eleven- and twelve-year-old boys. He and his friends were observing a raid over Senglea and witnessed, for example, how a bomb sliced off the roof of a local cinema.

When he went with his family to their apartment in Marsa Scala, he would steal away and go swimming around the wreck of the *Breconshire*. On one occasion, while they were out in a rowing boat and an enemy plane swooped over, they jumped out of the boat, turned it over and hid beneath it!

Godwin's family was fortunate that it could afford to eke out its rations with purchases on the black market. He remembers particularly 'an old guy' who kept a bath tub apparently full of wheat, but underneath there were cans of meat, which could be purchased for a considerable price. Meanwhile 1 lb of potatoes could cost as much as £1 Sterling (approximately £30 in modern terms). Nevertheless, he was regularly sent to pick up food from the Victory Kitchen on the corner of his road. This was supplemented by salads, grapes and harrope, a beat grown for horse food. The family did most of its cooking on barbecues fuelled with wood from the bomb sites.

Appendix VIII:
Biographies of Key Figures

⟫•⟨

Acheson, Andrew (1895–1959): Colonial Office 1920. Assistant Secretary in 1938. Assistant Secretary, Cabinet Office, 1948–57.

Beak, Major General Danie (1891–1957): MC with Bar, DSO and VC. Commander RNVR, 1914–1918. GOC Malta, 1942.

Bonham-Carter, General Sir Charles (1876–1955): Served South African War and First World War. Director of Staff Duties, War Office, 1927–31. Commander 4th Division, 1931–33. Governor of Malta, 1936–40.

Burrough, Vice Admiral Sir Harold Martin (1888–1977): Midshipman 1904. Specialized in gunnery. Assistant Chief Naval Staff. Commander of Force X in the *Pedestal* Convoy, August 1942. Vice Admiral 1943.

Cunningham, Viscount Admiral Andrew Browne, of Hyndhope. Admiral of the Fleet and leading British Naval Commander in the Second World War (1883–1963): Midshipman 1899. Commanded the destroyer *Scorpion* 1911–18. Captain 1920. Commanded battleship *Rodney*, 1929. Admiral and C-in-C Mediterranean, 1939. First Sea Lord, 1943–45.

Ford, Admiral Sir Wilbraham (1880–1964): Commanded *Royal Oak*, 1929. Rear Admiral, 1932. Vice Admiral Superintendent Malta, 1937–40. FOIC Malta, 1940–41. Admiral 1941.

Dobbie, General Sir William (1879–1964): Cadet at Woolwich. Joined the Royal Engineers. Served in the South African War. Staff College, 1912–13. Staff Officer 1915–18. Engaged in Staff work at the War Office, Aldershot and Western Command, 1920–28. Commanded Infantry Brigade, Cairo, 1928–32. GOC Singapore and Malaya, 1935–39. Retired August 1939. May 1940, Acting Governor, Malta, May 1940. April 1941–May 1942, Full Governor. Retired 1942.

Gort, Lord John (1886–1946): VC 1918. CIGS, 1937–39. C-in-C British Expeditionary Force, France, 1939–40. Governor of Gibraltar, 1940–42. Governor of Malta, 1942–44.

Jackson, Sir Edward (1886–1961): Called to the Bar 1908. Attorney General, Tanganyika, 1924–29, and of Ceylon, 1929–36. Retired 1936. Legal Secretary, Malta, 1937–40. Lieutenant Governor, Malta 1940–43. Chief Justice, Cyprus, 1945–51. Chief Judge, British Zone, Germany, 1953. UK member of commission to review sentences for German war crimes 1955–57.

Kesselring, Air Field Marshal, Albert (1896–1960): Joined Imperial German Army in 1914. Brigade Adjutant and General Staff Officer, 1914–18. Continued to serve as Staff Officer, 1919–33. Transferred to the Luftwaffe in October 1933. Commanded Luftwaffegruppe I (later Luftflotte I) 1940–43. C-in-C South and Commander of German forces in Italy 1943. C-in-C German forces on the Western Front March 1945.

Leatham, Admiral Edward (1886–1954): Captain 1924. Vice Admiral 1939. FOIC Malta, 1942–43. Deputy Governor, 1943. Retired 1946.

Park, Sir Keith, Air Vice Marshal (1892–1982): Born in New Zealand. Started work with the Union Steamship Company as a Cadet Purser in 1911. Joined the Army as a gunner in 1914. Royal Flying Corps in 1917. Between the wars he passed through the RAF Staff College, become air attaché in Buenos Aires and was a commanding officer at one of Britain's peacetime fighter stations. Appointed C-in-C of 11 Group, Fighter Command in 1939. Commanded squadrons in Egypt in 1941. AOC, Malta in 1942 and South East Asia in 1944–45. After the war returned to New Zealand.

Pughe, Sir Hugh (1894–1981): Joined Royal Engineers, 1915. Royal Flying Corps, 1917. Squadron Leader, 1929. Commanded No. 9 Bomber Group 1938. Senior Staff Officer of No. 2 Bomber Group, May 1940. Commander of RAF Mediterranean at Malta, June 1941. Senior Staff Officer, Middle East, July 1942. Air Chief Marshal, 1951. Retired 1953.

Appendix VIII

Scobie, Lieutenant General Sir Ronald (1893–1969): Major General 1941. GOC, Tobruk Fortress, 1941. GOC Malta, August 1942–44. GOC Greece, 1944–46.

Scobell, Major General, Sir John (1879–1955): Staff Officer, 1914–18. War Office, 1928–30. Retired 1939. GOC Malta, 1939–42. Lieutenant of the Tower of London, 1942–45.

Somerville, Admiral Sir James (1882–1949): Joined RN in 1897. Wireless specialist. Director of Signals, 1925–27. Vice Admiral, 1937. C-in-C East Indies, 1938. Commanded Force H at Gibraltar, 1940–42. Admiral of the Fleet, 1945.

Strickland, Mabel (1899–1988): Journalist and politician. The daughter of Lord Strickland, former Prime Minister of Malta. Editor of the *Times of Malta* during the Second World War. Led the Progressive Constitutional Party during the 1950s. Elected to the Maltese Parliament in 1962. She is buried in the Cathedral of Mdina.

Syfret, Vice Admiral, Sir Edward Neville (1889–1972): Joined RN, 1974. Gunnery officer in the North Sea in First World War. Between the wars Fleet Gunnery Officer, Mediterranean Fleet. Captain Naval Gunnery School at Davenport. Commander of *Caradoc*, *Ramillies* and *Rodney*. Rear Admiral, 1940. Commander Force H,1942. Senior Officer Force F during *Pedestal*. Chief of Naval Staff, 1943.

Vian, Admiral, Sir Philip (1894–1968): Fought at Jutland, 1916. Served in destroyers, 1919–36. Commanded 15th Cruiser Squadron in the Mediterranean, 1942. Vice Admiral, 1945. Admiral of the Fleet, 1952.

Appendix IX: Bibliography

1 Primary Sources

a) The National Archives (formerly the Public Record Office) at Kew contain all the official Colonial Office, War Office, Air Ministry and Admiralty records dealing with Malta for the period of the siege, 1940–42. I have found the following files of particular use and have heavily drawn on them:

Material dealing with preparations for a possible war with Italy in late 1938 to May 1940 may be found in the following files of the Colonial Office:

PRO CO 323/1552/17, CO 323/1657/92, CO 323/1657/94, CO 323/1657/94, CO 323/1592/55, CO 323/1658/15, CO 323/1658/17, CO 323/1866/12, CO 926/1/9, CO 926/1/11.CO 926/1/12, CO 926/1/16.

Material dealing with different aspects, such as propaganda, financial compensation, the morale of the Maltese, education, health, welfare, construction of shelters, the impact of enemy action, the government of Malta, including matters to do with the appointment of Governors, supply etc., once hostilities with Italy have broken out may be found in the following files:

PRO CO 323/1787, CO323/1737/10, CO/323/1839, CO 323/1731/23, CO 323/1839, CO323/1866/12; CO926/1/9, CO926/1/11, CO926/1/12, CO926/1/14, CO926/1/16; CO852/358/18, 852/358/19; CO967/89; CO968/7/90; CO968/7/10, CO968/7/11, CO/968/7/12, CO968/35/15, CO968/39/6, CO968/42/6, CO968/95/2, CO968/95/3, CO968/106/6; CO875/1/7, CO875/1/8, CO875/4/19, CO875/7/1, CO875/7/2, CO875/14/1, CO875/14/2, CO875/14/3; CO1045/178, CO/1045/347; CO158/533, CO158/534, CO158/537, CO158/538,

Appendix IX

CO158/539, CO158/540, CO158/541, CO158/542, CO852/345/10, CO852/1–5, CO852/364/4, CO852/406/1, CO852/407/7.

Matters concerning the supply of Spitfires in 1942 and Dobbie's replacement by Gort:

PRO. PREM 3/266/4, 3/266/1.

Questions of supply, convoys and naval matters in Malta:

PRO ADM 571/42, ADM 1/11981, 11079, 11969, 12208, 15739; ADM 199/ 108, 109, 413, 1242, 1243, 1244, 2008, 2406, ADM 223/340, 335, 342, 454, 519, 524, 529. 534, 537. 540. 541572; ADM 1/ 300, 11886; ADM 116/4539, 4061; ADM 119/424; ADM 195/70; ADM 338/51.

War Office correspondence with the Governor and matters concerning the Army in Malta:

PRO WO 106/, 2110, 2111,2112, 2113, 2114, 3062,3065, 3066, 3067, 3068 ; WO 32/2413, 2414, 14213; WO 195/1766; WO 193/62, 513, 618. WO 22/513; WO 216/129.

Material concerning the air defence of Malta:

PRO AIR20/2428; AIR 23/1200, 1201; AIR 24/908, 909; AIR 20/914.

b) The Imperial War Museum, London

The Imperial War Museum, London, has a large holding of private papers belonging to service personnel and civilians, who were in Malta during the siege. The following collections were particularly useful:

PP/MCR/C40 (Second Lieutenant J.Q. Hughes)

95/5/1 (Lt-Cmd. M.S. Blois-Brooke RNVR)

84/28/1 (Principal Matron, Miss M.E. Buckingham)

PP/MCR/ C45 (Squadron Leader J.M.V. Carpenter)

99/75/1 (Capt. E.D. Norman R.N.)

84/50/1 (W. Scicluna)

90/38/1 (Captain G.C. Blundell)

92/27/1 (H.E. Venn)

86/11/1 (Commander D.E. Barton)

91/29/1 (Surgeon Captain E. Heffernan)

84/13/1 (Sir Hannibal Scicluna)

02/8/1 (A.W. Rowntree)

91/1/1 (F.K. Rodgers)

75/25/1 (Col. L.H.M. Westropp)

92/30/1 (Norah Jane Goreing)

The Siege of Malta

87/23/1 (Gunner H. Fleming)
82/17/1 (Lt. Gen. Sir Ronald Scobie)

Secondary Sources
There are literally hundreds of books on the siege of Malta, 1940–42. I found the following very useful in writing this book:

OFFICIAL ACCOUNTS
The Air Battle of Malta, London, HMSO, 1944
Richard, D. and Hilary, S., *Royal Air Force, 1939–1940*, HMSO, 1957
Playfair, I., *The Mediterranean and Middle East*, Vols I, II, III and IV, HMSO, 1954–1960
S. Roskill, S., *The War at Sea*, Vols I and II. HMSO. 1956–60

OTHER PUBLISHED SOURCES
Attard, J., *The Battle of Malta: An Epic Story of Suffering and Bravery*, William Kimber, 1980
Barnett, C., *Engage the Enemy More Closely*, London, Hodder and Stoughton, 1991
Barnham, D., *One Man's Window*, William Kimber, 1956
Boffa, C., *The Illustrious Blitz: Malta in Wartime, 1940–41*, Progress Press, 1995
Bradford, E., Siege: *Malta 1940–43*, Hamish Hamilton, 1985
Chaplin, H., *The Queen's Own Royal West Kent Regiment, 1920–1950*, Michael Joseph, 1954
Dobbie, S., *Faith and Fortitude. The Life and Work of Sir William Dobbie*, P.E. Johnston, 1979
Douglas-Hamilton, J., *The Air Battle for Malta: The Diaries of a Spitfire Pilot*, Wrens Park, 2000
Dunning, C., *Combat Units of the Regia Aeronautica*, Air Research Publications, 1988
Dunning, C., *Courage Alone: The Italian Air Force, 1940–43*, Hikoki, 1998
Fussell, P., *Understanding and Behaviour in the Second World War*, OUP, 1989
Gilchrist, Major R.T., *Malta Strikes Back: The Story of 231 Infantry Brigade*, Gale and Ploden, 1946
Hamlin, J., *Military Aviation in Malta, 1915–1993*, GMS Enterprises,

Appendix IX

1994

Holland, J., *Fortress Malta: An Island Under Siege, 1940–43*, Orion, 2003

Hogan, George, *Malta: The Triumphant Years, 1940–1943*, Hale, 1978

Johnston, T., *Tattered Battlements: A Fighter Pilot's Diary*, William Kimber, 1985

Kesselring, A., Field Marshal, *The Memoirs of Field Marshal Kesselring*, William Kimber, 1953

Leslie Oliver, R., *Malta at Bay*, Hutchinson, 1942

Lloyd, Air Marshal, Sir Hugh, *Briefed to Attack: Malta's Part in African Victory*, Hodder and Stoughton, 1949

Lucas, P. and Lucas, L., *The Thorn in Rommel's Side: Six Months That Turned the War*, Stanley Paul, 1992

Micallef, J., *When Malta Stood Alone*, Malta 1981

Price, Dr A., *The Luftwaffe Databook*, Greenhill Books, 1997

Rogers, A., *Battle Over Malta: Aircraft Losses and Crash Sites, 1940–42*, Sutton, 2000

Shankland, P. and Hunter, A., *Malta Convoy*, Collins, 1961

Shores, C. and Cull, B., *Malta: The Hurricane Years 1940–41*, Grub Street, 1987

Shores, C., Cull, B. and Malizia, N., *Malta: The Spitfire Year, 1942*, Grub Street,1991

Smith, P., *Pedestal: The Malta Convoy of August 1942*, William Kimber, 1970

Smith, P., *Battles of the Malta Striking Forces*, Ian Allen, 1974

Spooner, T., *Supreme Gallantry: Malta's Role in the Allied Victory, 1939–1945*, John Murray, 1996

Thomas, D., *Malta Convoys*, Leo Cooper, 1999

Turner, J., *Persicope Patrol*, Harrap, 1957

Williams, D.L., *Siege*, Ian Allan, 1993

Wingate, J., *The Fighting Tenth: The Tenth Submarine Flotilla and the Siege of Malta*, Leo Cooper, 1991

Wismayer, J.M., *History of Kings Own Malta Regiment*, Said International Ltd, 1989

Woodman, R., *Malta Convoys, 1940–43*, John Murray, 2000

Vella, P., *Malta: Blitzed But Not Beaten*, Progress Press, 1985

Appendix X: Glossary

AA	Anti-Aircraft
AOC	Officer Commanding
ARP	Air Raid Precaution
Bn	Battalion
C-in-C	Commander-in-Chief
DMO	District Medical Officer
Det	Detachment
E-Boat	Italian motor torpedo boat
Flt.	Flight
FOIC	Flag Officer in Command
KOMR	Kings Own Malta Regt
ML	Minelayer
MTB	Motor Torpedo Boat
PO	Protection Officer
RA	Royal Artillery
RAOC	Royal Army Ordnance Corps
RASC	Royal Army Service Corps
RDF	Radio Direction Finding (Radar)
Regt	Regiment
RMA	Royal Malta Artillery
RPO	Regional Protection Officer
Sqd	Squadron
U-boat	German Submarine
VAM	Vice Admiral, Malta

Index

The Siege of Malta

Index

The Siege of Malta

Index